TURNING HEADS AND CHANGING MINDS

Transcending IT Auditor Archetypes

Turning Heads and Changing Minds

Transcending IT Auditor Archetypes

CHONG EE

IT Governance Publishing

Every possible effort has been made to ensure that the information contained in this book is accurate at the time of going to press, and the publisher and the author cannot accept responsibility for any errors or omissions, however caused. Any opinions expressed in this book are those of the author, not the publisher. Websites identified are for reference only, not endorsement, and any website visits are at the reader's own risk. No responsibility for loss or damage occasioned to any person acting, or refraining from action, as a result of the material in this publication can be accepted by the publisher or the author.

Apart from any fair dealing for the purposes of research or private study, or criticism or review, as permitted under the Copyright, Designs and Patents Act 1988, this publication may only be reproduced, stored or transmitted, in any form, or by any means, with the prior permission in writing of the publisher or, in the case of reprographic reproduction, in accordance with the terms of licences issued by the Copyright Licensing Agency. Enquiries concerning reproduction outside those terms should be sent to the publisher at the following address:

IT Governance Publishing
IT Governance Limited
Unit 3, Clive Court
Bartholomew's Walk
Cambridgeshire Business Park
Ely
Cambridgeshire
CB7 4EA
United Kingdom
www.itgovernance.co.uk

First published in the United Kingdom in 2013
by IT Governance Publishing

ISBN 978-1-84928-384-7

ABOUT THE AUTHOR

Chong Ee did not start out being an IT auditor; he became one after donning the hats of an IT management consultant and a business analyst. Over time, Chong worked on both sides: external auditing and in-house compliance. In 2012, he returned to systems implementation for cloud apps after eight years in Sarbanes–Oxley compliance. He has spoken at conferences hosted by the MIS Training Institute (MISTI), Information Systems Audit and Control Association (ISACA), Institute of Internal Auditors (IIA) and Society of Corporate Compliance and Ethics (SCCE), and has had articles published in the *Internal Auditor* magazine and ISACA and Information Systems Security Association (ISSA) journals. His first book, *Compliance by Design: IT Controls that Work*, was published by IT Governance Publishing in September 2011. Chong is an active Certified Information Systems Auditor (CISA) and Certified in the Governance of Enterprise IT (CGEIT).

ACKNOWLEDGEMENTS

Special thanks to Vicki Utting, Angela Wilde, Sophie Sayer and Alan Calder at IT Governance Publishing, and to Antonio Velasco, CEO, Sinersys Technologies, Chris Evans, ITSM specialist, and Giuseppe G. Zorzino CISA CGEIT CRISC, Security Architect, for their useful contributions during the review process.

For Michael

CONTENTS

INTRODUCTION

The idea for this book came to me when I was doing the conference circuit. Several times a year, I scheduled time away from work to speak at audit and compliance conferences. Starting in the local San Francisco Bay Area, I branched out to out-of-state locales. My focus was IT audits: I covered anything from general computer and application controls to audit communications and client delivery. Countless red-eye flights (and sleepless nights) later, it occurred to me that participants from varied industries often voiced the same need: how can IT auditors evolve from traditional finger-pointing roles to become convincing partners with business and technology counterparts? Can we adopt a behavioral pattern to excel at building or sustaining client relationships? Have we omitted a detail during audit planning or on-site fieldwork? Is there yet another newer technology that we need to familiarize ourselves with to uncover risks that are of meaning and value? Like my peers, I kept looking elsewhere – searching for that elusive nugget of information that could yet make a difference – not knowing that all this frantic activity only serves to take us farther away from discovering any real driver of change.

To truly begin to break out of ascribed roles or stereotypes, we need to look within, rather than without, unflinchingly, as it were, at underlying motivations and thoughts, and recognize that our audit findings are as much a product of our external environment as our inner paradigms and assumptions. Naturally, all this is easier said than done. Few audit books or articles even acknowledge, let alone discuss at length, our subjective realities. Of those that scratch at the surface, Sawyer's *Internal Auditing* and K. H. Spencer's *The Internal Auditor at Work* come to mind. The former acknowledges the auditor's dilemma of having to build rapport with auditees to elicit findings and yet report any gaps or wrongdoings to their managing supervisors. The latter shines a light on unofficial audit agenda such as wanting to looking good and not being inconvenienced.

By looking within, I had to be brutally honest and willing to undertake a hard, unbiased examination of my own audit experiences in particular, as well as the trajectory my career has traversed in general. I did not start out being an IT auditor and in fact only became one after wearing the hats of an IT management consultant and business analyst. I recall with less than fond memories my first days auditing operating systems and applications. Because it was my first gig, I had to go back and forth with the client even after the engagement ended to respond more fully to review comments on my audit workpapers. By mid-year, I gained confidence in my new role. I was often the systems auditor assigned to daunting projects that I in turn gained great satisfaction in uncovering findings like no other. There was a certain level of freedom, not to mention luxury, in having a job in which one's foremost responsibility was to ask questions, meet with stakeholders from multiple functions, and map enterprise-wide processes from start to finish.

By the time Sarbanes–Oxley was in effect, I was in the right place at the right time: I made the move from public auditing to in-house SOX (Sarbanes–Oxley Act 2002) compliance, managing entity, business, and technology internal controls across the organization. My initial entry was not unlike a rude shock one experiences upon diving into icy water. With less than six months to achieve compliance, I did not have the privilege of swooping in annually or quarterly for update audits; if anything, compliance was often painstaking, an everyday process of working with key stakeholders to tweak and refine internal controls as well as interfacing with external auditors to meet regulatory requirements. In the latest turn of events, I returned to systems implementation after eight years in compliance.

In reflecting upon my journey, I realize that my personal experiences are part of a larger collective pattern. Archetypes are images of thoughts, feelings, and behaviors that reflect the accumulated experience of all human beings. Swiss psychologist, and a key founder of modern psychology, Carl Jung, describes archetypes as primordial imprints located within a collective unconscious, a universal blueprint that reflects the common experiences of humanity in every person. Just as scientists build models to understand elusive or intangible realities, archetypes can be glimpsed through archetypal images. Thus, our journey into archetypes is in part an attempt to discover essence through form. At any point in time, we can carry a multitude of archetypes; one may be dominant whilst the others lie dormant. Jungian psychiatrist, Jean Shinoda Bolen, likened archetypes to members of a board meeting. In our context, think of archetypes as different members of an audit committee. Which one has the loudest say? Which ones have you ignored? In working with archetypal images, we need to take care not to pigeonhole specific individuals or romanticize specific roles. I am reminded of the following writing in Thomas Merton's journal:[1]

What you observe ... by becoming what we want it to be, it takes a disguise which we have decided to impose upon it.

The word archetype derives from the Latin noun *archetypum*, conveying beginning, origin, pattern, model, and type. In identifying various IT auditor archetypes, it is my intent to shine a light on the prescribed roles we play. We play these roles in lieu of undertaking richer, fuller, individual journeys. Many IT auditors, for instance, continue to subscribe to the idea that being effective means having to be critical and confrontational at all costs if only to prevail over their clients' thinking or behavior. Back in my early days of IT auditing, the number of audit findings uncovered was a personal and professional benchmark of success. To break out of ascribed roles or stereotypes, we need to re-examine our inner paradigms from a third-person perspective: the stories we tell ourselves, the roles we script, and the plots we weave. Consider the following archetypal responses to a difficult client:

He has something to hide – Skeptic

Let's revisit our assumptions to dig deeper beneath the surface – Sleuth

He needs to understand underlying risks – Protector

There must be a better way to mitigate risks and meet performance goals – Partner.

How we see the world is driven by the archetypes we unwittingly invite in. When driven by a dominant

---

[1] Thomas Merton, *A Search for Solitude: Searching for the Monk's True Life*, New Directions Publishing Corp., New York (1996), p. 190.

archetype, we circumscribe our reality and close ourselves to a plethora of perspectives that avail themselves to us. "What we experience depends on how we conceive," proclaims Elémire Zolla in *Archetypes.*[2] Consider how an IT auditor's predispositions may hinder her from picking up contextual clues in the client environment; or how the self-righteousness of another may blind him from seeking unlikely allies in the process of augmenting internal controls. As you might imagine, shedding all pretenses of one's persona – how one thinks one should, and has hitherto, appeared to oneself and before the world – can be a welcome relief. Yet, most of us remain blissfully unaware that the individual personas we assert are really driven by a larger collective.

In working with archetypes, we also have to come face to face with our shadows. What are shadows? When clients think of the archetypal Skeptic in auditors, they are likely to dwell on the Critic shadow. Questions, questions, questions – this ever-pressing need to answer them the best way you know how and hoping against all odds that you would not be faulted for giving the wrong answer. Imagine a different scenario: showing up at a client site and hearing no, no, no – an emphatic denial to the presence of controls. Hearing this, what is your likely response? You cannot believe your luck chalking this up as yet another low-hanging audit find? Or do you find your curiosity piqued enough to dig deeper?

Shadows are unpleasant, unsavory, even repugnant aspects of ourselves that we are hesitant to acknowledge or confront. Instead, we deal with this in a couple of ways:

---

[2] Elémire Zolla, *Archetypes: The Persistence of Unifying Patterns*, Harcourt, New York (1982).

- Suppress the shadow even as it continues to guide our actions behind the scenes, or
- Deny the shadow by projecting it on others and becoming critical of them.

In either approach, the more you suppress or deny, the more your shadow taunts you in sudden flare-ups or antagonisms. Take the Skeptic archetype as an example. By over-identifying with it, you risk taking on the Critic shadow; when deprived of it, you come into the Dogmatic shadow.

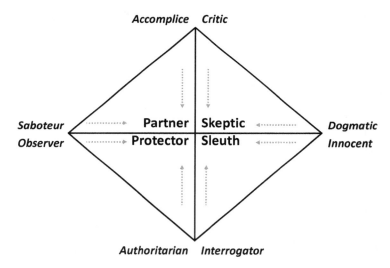

Figure 1: Archetypes and shadows

In this book we will cover four auditor archetypes: Skeptic, Sleuth, Protector, and Partner. Archetypal shadows reside on opposite poles of an archetypal spectrum (see Figure 1). The vertical axis represents an over-identification with a specific archetype, the horizontal axis an under-identification of the same archetype. I have adapted the three-part archetypal structure used by Robert Moore and Douglas Gillette[3] to describe its bipolar shadow system. In the Skeptic archetype for instance, the Critic represents the top dog or aggressor role and the Dogmatic represents the underdog or victim role. Another way of thinking about the opposite shadows is to see them as active and passive poles, the former as one doing unto others and the latter as others doing unto oneself.

This book is divided into three parts. In *Part I*, we will familiarize ourselves with the landscape of auditor archetypes and the shadows they cast. In *Part II*, we will look at ways and means to transcend these archetypes. In *Part III*, we will revisit the nature of auditing in the context of the archetypes presented.

Transcendence is not simply about taking on positive aspects of a particular archetype or shuttling from one archetype to another. It is more about embracing archetypes, and, in particular, our shadows to unify seeming polar opposites. It has less to do with fighting the good fight, declaring victory of good versus evil and more to do with questioning whether the fight is even worth fighting at all, and rising above the fray. As we shall see, archetypes are neither all good nor all bad; what matters is *how* we interact with them.

By failing to recognize the archetypal attributes we unconsciously take on, we limit the magnetic field of possibilities available to us. Archetypes have been compared to a magnet beneath a sheet of paper. Strewn

---

[3] Robert Moore and Douglas Gillette, *King Warrior Magician Lover: Recovering the Archetypes of the Mature Masculine*, HarperCollins Publishers, New York (1990).

above, iron filings take on the lines of the underlying magnetic force. Being caught in an archetypal pattern is like running on auto pilot, playing out tired dramas seen in client negotiations over audit findings, rather than developing any true awareness of the client's internal control environment. If, on the other hand, you are willing to step outside of yourself and loosen your grip on the roles you have acquired, you stand poised to realize your full potential.

PART I: ARCHETYPES

CHAPTER 1: THROUGH THE EYES OF THE SKEPTIC

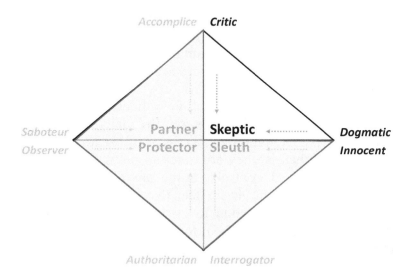

Figure 2: Skeptic archetype and shadows

Our journey begins with the Skeptic archetype (see Figure 2). The first step is arguably the hardest. To step into the unknown requires an equal measure of foolhardiness and willingness to let go. What of, you ask. Old habits, fixations, and illusions, though in no particular sequence; controls that appear to operate year after year; reviews performed even as no exceptions ever get identified. Management signs off on the dotted line and the company attains an A on the audit scorecard. The auditor as Skeptic questions this status quo: how can controls remain static in spite of organizational, system, and process change?

Conversely, when faced with a client with a dearth of internal controls, the auditor as Skeptic asks: really? If there were no controls, how would the right product get delivered in the right way to the right customer? Surely, there is some form of check and balance.

I have had clients who readily admit to the sheer absence of reviews. Yet when quizzed about the accuracy or validity of their deliverables – whether these are monthly full backups or periodic access configurations – they open up to a whole slew of procedures employed to validate their work – automated email notifications on the daily backup job status; the reconciliation of access profiles to headcount reports. Nonetheless, they are quick to point out that these are not formalized controls. Some are even resistant to labeling them as controls for fear that they would have to perform above and beyond to evidence control operating effectiveness, distracting them from the deliverable at hand. Through the work of the auditor as Skeptic, these seemingly informal controls may yet emerge to see the light of day.

What can go wrong?

As auditors, controls form our everyday language. It can be hard to see the negative associations tied to a control. Clients' aversion to controls is not uncommon, especially in the early days of Sarbanes–Oxley, when anything that so much as creaked was subsumed under the umbrella of compliance. From a client's perspective, the mere mention of a control may convey underlying meanings of mistrust, weakness, or even ineptitude.

Questions, questions, questions – these auditors are unbearable.

1: Through the Eyes of the Skeptic

To the undiscerning eye, the Skeptic archetype can appear negative, doubtful, or pessimistic. Yet, it speaks to the inquisitiveness within us, the ability to not accept something at face value but to find out more. To client personnel used to performing daily routines, the onslaught of questions may at first appear intrusive, yet they are necessary in encouraging them to see the same environment with a fresh pair of eyes. From the auditor's perspective, taking on the Skeptic archetype can require a great deal of bravery and persistence.

There were times that I was literally scared to death and I had to find a way to push forward through my fear[4]

At a Joint National Conference, an annual three-day event organized by the American Society of Women Accountants and the American Woman's Society of CPAs, Cynthia Cooper recounted her experience of running the internal audit department at WorldCom and detecting a discrepancy in the company's third-quarter results. She and her team uncovered more than $3 billion in fraud and ultimately led the US Senate to add Section 404, the assessment of internal controls, to the Sarbanes–Oxley Act.

As with other archetypes, challenging clients or circumstances often encourage the auditor to embrace the Skeptic archetype. For instance, when sent to audit a recently acquired foreign start-up subsidiary, the challenge can be getting auditees to understand the value of internal controls on the one hand, whilst attempting to identify pertinent risks in a different business environment on the

---

[4] David M. Katz and Julia Homer, "WorldCom Whistle-blower Cynthia Cooper", *CFO Magazine*, February 1, 2008.

other. By repressing the Skeptic archetype, however, the auditor readily gives away her responsibility and power to the auditee. I have seen auditors who cowered under the wrath of imposing clients, losing their train of thought or settling with glib general responses that sidestep the issue at hand.

How can you possibly know about our operations? You function in an ivory tower.

Often, the self-worth of the auditor is placed into question. By their very nature, auditors do not gain knowledge by doing (*praxis*) or creating (*poiesis*) but by inquiry (*theoria*). It does not help their credibility if they are fresh out of school or have only worked in auditing since graduation. Auditors who are best able to withstand the barrage of defensive, even disparaging, remarks and stand their ground are those who remain collected and composed under pressure. By explaining the rationale and context of their questions, they are able to convince their clients that they are acting in good faith. A key ingredient of success is, ironically enough, a non-attachment to outcome. The more the auditor seeks to prevail over the auditee, arguing incessantly, even vehemently, the more the auditee fortifies her armor. If on the other hand, the auditor is willing to listen to the auditee rather than insist on her position, unexpected finds await.

Another contributing factor is a genuine intention to help the client mitigate risk, rather than seek to appear competent or discover findings for findings sake. Auditors with less than honorable intentions often unwittingly project self-mistrust on the auditee. When the auditee responds with skepticism, that is, asks a question to seek clarification, the auditor lashes out in self-defense or insists on the rigor of audit methodology.

Dogs bark at every one they do not know – Heraclitus[5]

By denying the Skeptic archetype, the auditor can project it onto the auditee and take on the role of the Dogmatic. Rather than get at the root cause of a process breakdown, the dialogue can easily degenerate into scapegoating and blame. An insistent Dogmatic audit style often masks self-doubt and ambivalence. A desire to hide one's relative lack of knowledge in a new system can be projected onto the other so that the auditee rather than the auditor appears to be hiding something. On the other hand, the Skeptic archetype can be overtaken by the shadow of the Critic. A preoccupation with right versus wrong, combined with an audit approach mirroring the approach of a Salem witch hunt, casts the auditor as cold, callous, and calculating, someone to shun rather than to rely on as a voice of reason. There is a certain level of superiority that the Critic carries in casting judgments. Look at any audit finding and words such as "should" abound. We are all familiar with the caricature type who always interrupts, never listens. She relishes in disrupting one's train of thought or poking holes in one's logic. She enjoys the freedom or power that comes with casting others in a critical light. Yet, this very freedom or power enjoyed at the expense of others seems oddly hollow. The act of criticism conceals an innate fear to appear ignorant, uncertain, or wrong. Because of this fear, the auditor as Critic is more known for her inaction than

---

[5] Heraclitus, "Fragments of Heraclitus" (1912), available at: *http://en.wikisource.org/wiki/Fragments_of_Heraclitus*.

action; more a hairsplitter than a doer, she is quick to dispense with her critique yet slow in driving change. Similar to how a latent inferiority complex can underlie an outward superiority, as pointed out by Austrian psychotherapist, Alfred Adler, she easily takes offense against countering points of view and struggles to hang on to cherished beliefs and ideas. Here, the Critic mirrors the Dogmatic. Likewise, the Dogmatic mirrors the Critic by opposing any proposed change to pre-existing beliefs. The Critic over-identifies with the Skeptic archetypal energy; the Dogmatic is depleted of this very same archetypal energy. In one sense, although one reacts and the other deflects, both the Critic and the Dogmatic share a fear of the unknown. Against these polar opposites, the Skeptic walks the middle path.

A characteristic of the Skeptic is that she may be indecisive, uncertain, wavering. Caution and deliberate care can easily descend into unresponsiveness and inaction. In this regard, the Skeptic archetype requires the accompaniment of the Sleuth archetype to take action. Where the former emphasizes hypothesis forming, the latter emphasizes field validation. Other archetypes, such as the Protector, are useful in keeping the overzealous Critic at bay by focusing on the needs of the client. In turn, the Skeptic archetype is useful at each phase of our growth; it propels us to take on a different role whether it is graduating from the Protector to Partner archetypes or simply changing the outlook we have adopted or taken for granted over time.

To awaken the Skeptic archetype in us, we must be willing to embrace the ambiguity inherent in every situation. Take a client who approaches an auditor about tightening the segregation of duties in an enterprise application. The auditor can proceed to investigate the different configuration options within the application and uncover a new way to counterbalance automated controls with manual ones outside of the application. Here, she takes on the Sleuth and Protector archetypes. Alternatively, the auditee may start by asking why. Why would the segregation of duties in the application merit revisiting? Was there a change in personnel or business process? Whatever the case may be, the auditor as Skeptic does not take things for granted even if considered the norm or best practice. Tightening segregation of duties is music to an auditor's ears; the more controls we have, the merrier. Yet, it is only by asking why – understanding the context of the client need – can she truly see the root issue at hand. Through further probing, it may be that the problem lies with terminated employees still residing as ghost employees in the application. Tightening segregation is but one of the myriad of ways to mitigate risks of unauthorized access, yet it does not directly address the root cause and may even add to the application administration burden. A more effective fix may be fine-tuning the communication workflow amongst supervisors, human resources, and application administrators outside of the system.

The auditor as a Skeptic seeks to shed light on a situation. To embody the archetype fully, however, she needs to "turn the light around," a phrase commonly used in Taoist mediation. She needs to shine the light on herself, her own machinery of sensations, perceptions, thoughts, and judgments. When the Buddha lay dying, he told his disciples, "Be a lamp onto yourself!" To this end, the auditor as Skeptic needs to question her own mind. Like her auditees, she is inclined to operate on fixed beliefs that need to be aired, re-examined, and challenged periodically. Are all internal controls good? Can an excessiveness of internal controls actually lead to greater risk? Consider the multiple passwords we employ for varied login credentials. Some of us have resorted to writing these on a piece of paper or using the same password across all systems. To what extent has an over-reliance on password expiry, complexity, and change upon first time login – bread-and-butter access controls – contributed to a state where all is secure and consequently anything but? Every system is just as important, and as a result, no one system truly is.

The auditor as Skeptic is the first to admit, "I'm not so sure" or "hang on a minute," daring to ask the very questions that the Dogmatic refuses to acknowledge. She is not afraid to look bad by asking a silly question. As auditors, we sometimes forget our clients rely on us to look at the same situation with a fresh pair of eyes; engaged in the mundane rigmarole of the everyday, they are less likely to step outside of themselves to adopt a disinterested objective perspective. By loosening our grip on the need to appear in-the-know and credible, we may in effect gain greater client credibility. In practice, this is not easy. The client may react by being irritable. "Here we go again, helping to train the new crop of auditors," and "I already told you," are common client refrains. Yet, the Dogmatic or Critic in the auditee can awaken the Skeptic archetype in the auditor. A challenging client can encourage the auditor to probe deeper. Does the client have something to hide or gain? Is there an underlying assumption that was askew?

Conversely, I have drawn inspiration from observing Skeptic archetypes in others, whether they are chief financial officers (CFOs), managers, or line personnel. I have admired how they are able to step outside of group-think for a moment and ask the question teetering on everyone's lips: are we are still on the right path?

1: Through the Eyes of the Skeptic

Especially in projects with tight deadlines, when all eyes are focused upon the velocity at which we hurl ourselves towards our agreed goals, we run the risk of ending up like dumbfounded flies flattened against the glass at our own insistence. "We have always done it this way" or "we have no time for this" are common telltale symptoms of group behaviors or thinking that can benefit from a Skeptic archetype. Against a looming SOX compliance deadline, it can appear foolhardy to question whether attention should be spent on augmenting automated controls for a key financial application until one realizes the discussion would be moot in the absence of effective general computer controls like access administration and change management procedures that govern the very integrity of the application. Often, a question that appears to be a red herring is anything but. During the pre-implementation review of a system go-live, someone asked whether or not the proposed solutions would work with additional modules to be phased in at a later time. It turned out they would result in greater complexity and coupling issues over the long run. Eventually, a compromise was reached to delay go-live to incorporate the future phased modules into the initial rollout.

This fellow is wise enough to play the fool;
And to do that well craves a kind of wit.
He must observe their mood on whom he jests,
And, like the haggard, cheque at every feather
That comes before his eye. This is a practise
As full of labour as a wise man's art
For folly that he wisely shows is fit
But wise men, folly-fall'n, quite taint their wit.
– Viola from Shakespeare's *Twelfth Night*: Act 3, Scene 1

1: Through the Eyes of the Skeptic

The Skeptic archetype is not unlike the Fool archetype seen in literature and movies. The classic sidekick and a source of comic relief, they often act as the hero's conscience speaking the truth even if it appears awkward or unfashionable. I have been in situations where a seemingly trivial audit question is met with "I'm confused," gains momentum through "possibly," and swells to a crescendo of "why didn't we think of that?" When you combine an ability to put aside your ego to play the Fool with a non-attachment to outcome, you may very well succeed in walking the tightrope of the Skeptic, sidestepping the confrontational demeanor of the Critic on the one hand, and the self-righteousness of the Dogmatic on the other.

Exercise

Put on the Skeptic's cap. Challenge each of the following internal control clichés:

- Internal controls preclude real work from getting done
- Internal controls show a lack of trust
- Internal controls are hard to change.

As an example, see my opposing views below:

- Most clients understand internal controls as detective in nature; consequently, they slap on controls in downstream processes almost as an afterthought. When an error is detected in a review, the remediation is laborious and thus can be perceived to slow work down. However, preventive controls such as automated controls within the application can go a long way to prevent errors from happening. Rather than preclude real work from getting done, it can actually help us get real work done more effectively and efficiently.
- Trust is implicit in any professional relationship between employer and employee, management and personnel, customer and vendor. Internal controls, when properly designed, place emphasis on organizational processes, rather than individuals, to attain predictability in results. Thus when someone goes on vacation, or vendors change, controls remain in place to ensure that we still deliver with consistent results.
- Insofar as internal controls are about people and processes, the former are hard to change. By themselves, internal controls can be adapted to changing risks. However, just as old habits die hard, people are less willing to drop old behaviors even in the face of change. It is not uncommon that new applications are rolled out

with their core functionalities left untapped as users continue to rely on legacy manual controls.

Now, take the side of the client. For each internal control cliché, think of a scenario where it makes sense. The following come to mind:

- We are a small organization and have a lean headcount. The segregation of duties structure that you propose works for bigger organizations and is far too cost prohibitive for us to implement here. The normal processing of daily transactions would slow to a crawl.
- I'm not volunteering any more information. The last time you were here, you raised a bunch of issues thanks to my big mouth. When you left, my co-workers no longer trusted my work.
- Management is hesitant to drop this compensating control. We understand that the risks have been mitigated upstream by the new system. However, our external auditors have grown accustomed to our internal control design and rationale. Dropping this control would risk drawing any unwarranted attention.

CHAPTER 2: FORGING AHEAD WITH THE SLEUTH

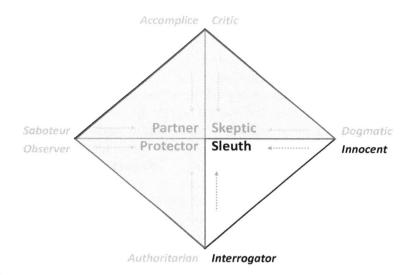

Figure 3: Sleuth archetype and shadows

As a kid, I was entranced by Miss Marple and Hercule Poirot. I spent summer vacations cooped up in my room combing through Agatha Christie's detective novels. Little did I know then that I would be manifesting a Sleuth archetype when auditing in the not so distant future. Whilst the Skeptic archetype is characterized by openness to uncertainty and ambiguity, the Sleuth archetype takes this a step farther, bridging an open disposition with tangible, concrete action. In this regard, the Sleuth archetype is about gathering clues, wading through seeming paraphernalia, piecing together parts of a puzzle to make a whole (see Figure 3).

Why did the auditor cross the road?
Because he looked in the file and that is what they did last year.

So much of auditing today, however, is driven by frameworks, practice aids, and checklists. A case in point is the nature of discussions that take place at audit conferences. Participants perk up when discussing the best framework to use, the fastest script to run or the most complete practice aide to meet audit and compliance requirements. These days, there are templates for everything – controls, testing, flowcharts, materiality assessment, and even findings. A preoccupation with completeness belies every hand gesticulation, intense gaze, and hushed tone: the compulsion to ask all the right questions to cover what is in scope, for fear that something gets missed in the briefest of moments. So intent have we become in going over, and consequently abiding by, our agenda, we ignore obvious clues or telltale signs. A favorite anecdote of mine is showing up at a client site armed with a chock load of workpapers. Sitting down with the Chief Information Officer (CIO), my first question was whether there were significant changes to the segregation of duties, to which he responded, "did you not see the rows of empty cubicles on your way to my office? We just had a layoff."

An underlying flaw with the use of templates and other shortcuts is an implicit acceptance in the universality of application. This surfaces when one hears conference attendees debate over the best controls to employ or absolute control must-haves. The answer, invariably an anti-climactic "it depends," is often met with an audience's disappointment. Yet, it is by putting aside our preconceptions that we start to embody the Sleuth archetype.

Mind has erected the objective outside world ... out of its own stuff.[6]

Most of the time, we remain unaware of how our inner thoughts, beliefs, and feelings can filter out key aspects of reality. It is well known in quantum physics that depending on the experiment performed, light can be perceived as both particles *and* waves. Thus, "how" we observe is just as important as "what" we observe. In emphasizing this importance in the Sleuth archetype, I am not as concerned with the plethora of qualitative or quantitative methods at our disposal as I am with the fundamental ways we become aware. Jung identified four functional types in consciousness: sensing (what is), thinking (what it is), feeling (what it is worth), and intuiting (a hunch). A dominating psychology function or set of functions determines how one reacts or responds to a given situation. According to Jung, a sensation type takes in details whereas intuitive types look at the big picture. Separately, in their book *Alive and Aware*, Sherod Miller, Elam Nunnally, and Dan Wackman developed the Awareness Wheel encompassing four areas of consciousness: sensations (what we perceive through our senses), interpretations (our

---

[6] Erwin Schrödinger, *Mind and Matter*, Cambridge University Press, Cambridge (1958).

assumptions or conclusions), feelings (our emotions), and desires (our wants)[7].

Consider the following scenario: you have been tasked to investigate the nature of recurring findings with a client. To what extent does your thinking (interpretation) or feelings shade your sense of the situation? Are you, for instance, more likely to see the client management as irresponsible, lazy, taking a cavalier approach to internal controls? Or are you more inclined to doubt your own audit recommendations; the findings recur simply because they are too difficult to execute or sustain. Your inner beliefs or predilections shape the nature of your inquiry. In the former, you are likely to seek out any inconsistencies in what client management conveys; in the latter, you are more open to exploring the inconsistencies within the audit recommendations. In either instance, you are too distracted by you – your thoughts, feelings, judgments – to notice cyclical changes in the client's business environment that make it all but difficult to implement the same solution in a consistent manner over the course of a single year, let alone year after year. Our instinctive response can be likened to seeing a rope in the dark and mistaking it for a snake. Described as *Adhyasa* in Sanskrit, we superimpose the snake on a real rope. Despite being an illusion, the snake exists in our mind, giving rise to real palpitations and angst.

Not always so[8]

---

[7] Sherod Miller, Elam W. Nunnally and Dan B. Wackman, *Alive and Aware: Improving Communications in Relationships*, Interpersonal Communication Programs, Inc., Evergreen, Colorado (October 1975).
[8] Shunryu Suzuki and Edward Espe Brown, *Not Always So: Practicing the True Spirit of Zen*, HarperCollins, New York (2003).

The key is auditing in the moment – seeing, hearing, and experiencing the present fully – as opposed to sifting it through an ever-growing catalog of memories, past encounters, and illusions. The temptation to rely on mental heuristics or shortcuts engenders logical fallacies such as anchoring biases. In a study of 395 experienced auditors, James Lloyd Bierstaker, James Hunton, and Jay Thibodeau discovered that auditors given a blank control matrix with a business flowchart outperformed those given a completed control matrix in the identification of missing controls.[9] Ironically, in the post-SOX world, the first commandment on the tip of every auditor's tongue is almost always, "show me your internal control matrix."

Abandoning preconceptions to cultivate awareness does not mean being an innocent. A negative pole of the Sleuth's shadow, the Innocent readily relinquishes power to the auditee, preferring instead to doodle over papers and numbers – child's play – rather than roll up their sleeves as part of their investigative work. Auditors seduced by the Innocent shadow archetype perform remote interviews with auditees who supply them readily packaged internal control evidence. They do not bother to independently corroborate details with others or validate the evidence firsthand. If auditees were to regurgitate or recycle the prior year's data, they would not have blinked! Periodic audits become ho-hum predictable affairs. Other times, the displayed naïveté comes across as contrived. Roped in by the script that gets

---

[9] James Lloyd Bierstaker, James Hunton, and Jay Thibodeau, "Do Client Prepared Internal Control Documentation and Business Process Flowcharts Help or Hinder an Auditor's Ability to Identify Missing Controls?", *AUDITING: A Journal of Practice & Theory*: Vol. 28, No. 1, (May 2009), pp. 79–94.

re-enacted year after year, auditees are conditioned to provide the same information and perform the ritual dance around audit findings each time. We hear "but that's how things get done around here" or "why reinvent the wheel." For these reasons, auditors as Innocents cast the audit profession in a bad light. In time, auditees become disillusioned with the overall audit process, seeing it as nothing more than a check-the-box exercise at best, an implicit collusion between auditors and management at worst. Deprived of the Sleuth's archetypal energies, the auditor as Innocent is really suppressing an inner desire to take action. When observing auditees actively engaged in troubleshooting an issue, she may find herself curiously envious. When she stays with this feeling, she begins to come to terms with her Innocent shadow.

Awareness means getting in touch with one's inner thoughts and desires and seeing how they can in turn direct one's senses, intentions, and actions. An auditor may be aware of boilerplate audit templates and lessons learned from past travails and, as a result, make inevitable comparisons of present circumstances with prior ones. Yet, by fully immersing herself in the investigative nature of her work, she discovers new ways of relating to the subject matter at hand, whether it may be an auditee, control evidence, or operational process. There was an especially difficult auditee I encountered in an application review. Despite countless reminders and subsequent meeting reschedules, I was unable to find time with her. Faced with a fast approaching project deadline, I was at my wit's end. When I finally ran into her at the water cooler, it was all I could do to keep from yelling. Seeing her harried look, I asked her how her day was. Hearing this, she lamented about missing deadlines (big surprise) and proceeded to reveal the manual workarounds introduced by the new application. What had up until then appeared to be a fairly successful application launch had a less than positive impact on her and her team. Because the application only accepted data input in highly regimented formats, they worked overtime to make sure that end-of-day entries were properly formatted for successful data imports the next day. Through a simple exchange at the water cooler, I not only gained a deeper appreciation of the application's lack of interface capability, I also came to understand how my ill-formed opinions of her, coupled with a desire to get the job done, precluded me from seeing the big picture. It took a mere moment of sheer serendipity to make this connection.

Most of us think of synchronicity as a coincidence in timing: two seemingly uncorrelated events coming together in an unexpected and, often delightful, manner. Jung clarified synchronicity as "a coincidence in time of two or more casually unrelated events which have the same or a similar meaning." Indeed, if there were no shared meaning, their fortuitous occurrence would have slipped right past from beneath our noses. In reviewing system access, I was making a mental note to request an updated organizational chart. At that very moment, who else should walk by but the human resources manager? In conducting my daily affairs, I often find that unexpected twists and turns reveal their meanings in retrospect. To excel as a Sleuth, the trick is to walk a fine line between grasping the workings of your inner world whilst participating in the spontaneous flow of the outer. Some of my most rewarding audits were the ones where I immersed myself fully in the client environment. Prior to on-site fieldwork, I did much research to prepare, reading up on prior year audit findings, operations manuals, or technical documentation on the systems in use. I showed up at the client facilities, however, with none of these in hand. Instead, I carried a blank notebook and made every attempt to reach out to key stakeholders. What I have found is that much of the homework I did upfront resonated enough in the background for me to pick up something of meaning in the foreground. In one instance, upon hearing about the manual approval processes in place for existing purchase orders (POs), I instantly thought of the specific application configuration to enable automation of PO approvals.

The light dove, in free flight cutting through the air the resistance of which it feels, could get the idea that it could do even better in airless space. (Immanuel Kant, *Critique Of Pure Reason*[10]

In embracing the Sleuth archetype, obstacles become part of the course. Rather than see obstacles as pesky inconveniences or barriers to be surmounted, look at them as a source of meaningful information. Is it trying to tell you to redirect your efforts elsewhere? Is it encouraging you to let go of specific beliefs or assumptions that do not apply in this situation? Is there some area you have missed? The Achilles heel of the Sleuth is the Interrogator archetype. Rather than trying to make sense of an uncooperative auditee or accelerated deadlines, the auditor seized by the Interrogator archetype attacks the perceived problem at hand. No prizes for guessing the outcome of this approach. Never mind the value of the audit, the auditee would be fortunate to end up with even a shred of dignity to her name. For most of us, it takes time to appreciate the

---

[10] Immanuel Kant, *Critique Of Pure Reason*, Henry G. Bohn, London (1855).

value of an arising obstacle. Had the client not been difficult, we would not have taken the opportunity to explain our audit sampling approach. Had the schedule remained unchanged, we would not have thought about auditing automated controls in the context of general computer controls rather than in isolation. Obstacles not only showcase what is on the outside; they also illuminate what is inside: parts of our personalities that we ignore or cling on to for fear of change. The Interrogator archetype sees obstacles as inherently negative, roadblocks that need to be steamrolled over. Unsuspecting auditees often complain about drive-by audits performed by auditors with a predetermined agenda. So focused are they on sticking to the script, they derail any bystander who stands in their path, consequently missing any clues crumbled in their wake.

The auditor possessed by the Interrogator archetype hears only what she wants to hear. Beneath the veneer of steely determination, there is an undertone of resistance, a non-acceptance with what is. The auditee may be trying to explain a process in further detail but wait, she interjects, that is not in scope. Propelled invisibly by a laundry list of items before her, she must make haste. In trying to cover everything, she accomplishes nothing. I have heard countless firsthand accounts from auditees who attempted to bring attention to an area of improvement only to be whisked along ever so expediently, their suggestions swept under the rug. It is an altogether very trying situation. Over time, they are conditioned to give monosyllabic answers, revealing begrudgingly only when pressed, maintaining stolid reticence at other times. Oddly enough, the Interrogator archetype arises almost as a defense mechanism whenever we feel vulnerable, fear of appearing ignorant or taking on the Innocent shadow archetype. When we hear client comments such as "surely you know what we're talking about" or "you must have seen this before," we can sometimes feel like the ground just gave way from beneath our feet. It can be hard not to feel discouraged. In response we erect formidable barriers: in our future interactions with current and future clients, we take on the role of the Interrogator as a pre-emptive attack, vacillating from one extreme to another, never quite finding the middle path. Like the Interrogator, an undertone of non-acceptance courses through the veins of the auditor as an Innocent. There is a reluctance to entertain, much less comprehend, real-life complexities or issues.

An object is known or unknown depending on whether or not it is reflected in the mind – Patanjali

We see color that is not absorbed and reflected by an object. When dominated by either the Interrogator or Innocent archetypal shadows, the auditor often misses the significance of what is unsaid. Although both archetypes differ – the former over-identifies with the Sleuth archetypal energy whereas the latter is depleted of this very same archetypal energy – both focus intently on what is said. Yet we know from personal experience that what is unsaid can often be more significant than what is said. A client may mention that they have installed an application firewall but omit to mention that it has not been configured properly to screen out false positives. Or an access review may be performed monthly but not against any validating support, such as an up-to-date active employee listing.

In the Sutras of Patanjali, he taught that for the moon to be reflected in a pool of water, every ripple needs to be stilled. For the auditor as Sleuth to pick up the unsaid, she needs to quiet her mind enough to reflect her client's environment. And so it is for the budding Sleuth in us as we venture forth into each different client environment. Are we going to see, hear, experience with unadulterated awareness? Are we more likely to judge by our exacting beliefs or hang on to past hurts?

Exercise

As a Sleuth, what we find is as much of a product of how we conduct our finds as what is out there. The manner in which we conduct our search is in turn driven by our senses, feelings, thoughts, and beliefs. The next time you show up at a client site, notice if you start to:

- Feel exasperated
- Fixate on your own agenda
- Become defensive
- Blame others.

At the end of each day, make a list of your activities. For each activity, assess to what extent it is:

- A compulsion to stick to the script
- An avoidance to handle uncertainty or complexity
- An unfolding of new possibilities
- A resistance to change.

For each activity, examine your underlying motivations or intentions:

- Find more issues than those identified from the prior year
- Wrap up audit engagements efficiently with no fuss
- Earn kudos from management
- Grasp the inner workings of a process from soup to nuts.

CHAPTER 3: SAFETY UNDER THE PROTECTOR

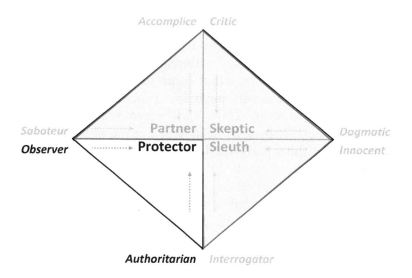

Figure 4: Protector archetype and shadows

When you turn the page in an IT audit or security textbook, words like attackers, hackers, cyber criminals pop up on almost every page. Budding IT auditors are trained to spot suspicious malicious insiders and guard against phishing, brute force, and other network attacks. The Protector archetype emerges when the Sleuth archetype identifies an area that needs securing (see Figure 4). Are our backups effective? Do we have a rollback plan for emergency program changes? Are controls in place for administrators or superusers? If not, what can be done? Management looks to auditors to propose a course of action and provide periodic updates on remedial efforts.

The general public sees an auditor as the modern-day corporate watchdog. Some even view her as an internal whistleblower. That said, when something does go terribly wrong and is reported by the media, as in the case of Enron, the auditor is not immune from blame. Why did you not find out sooner? Why did you not alert us? Did you not do your job? The same accusations abound with security breaches. Publicized ones that come to mind are the credit card data breaches at payment processors, Heartland Payment Systems, in 2008 and, more recently, Global Payment, in 2012. In both instances, questions were raised. Why did the third-party qualified security assessor (QSA) not uncover the breach in periodic audits? Were both institutions not certified as PCI compliant? What exactly were audited as internal controls? All this conspires to create an environment fraught with tension and blame. Flanked against this backdrop, it is not hard to see how some auditors never quite embrace the Protector archetype, favoring instead its shadow archetypes.

An auditor is a man who watches the battle from the safety of the hills and then comes down to bayonet the wounded –
Sir Charles Lyell, 1797–1875, American accountant

The auditor as mere loudspeaker or mouthpiece may be an unfair exaggeration but it certainly characterizes the auditor possessed by the Observer shadow archetype. Under the pretext of maintaining independence and objectivity, she skirts issues at hand, making a brief appearance periodically to obtain updates on the remediation performed. To auditees, she is an independent agent who swoops in, reports on issues, and conveniently skips away to the next target, leaving the rest of the organization to clean up the mess. Behind her detached demeanor lies an unwillingness to deal with the messiness that life deals us in spades.

The identification of excessive access, for instance, is but the first step. The hard work lies in securing a feasible working solution. Boilerplate audit recommendations typically propose that management review system access periodically, say every quarter, only to have auditors returning the following year to observe the same recurring concern. "You know auditors; they *have* to find something," is a common client lament, but it belies a perception that the thing found is much ado about nothing, or, if it is not, nothing could be done about it. Having management review access in a detective manner is like applying a Band-Aid to a festering wound. The recommendation treats surface symptoms rather than root causes. If access were not granted in an appropriate manner, excessive access is but a foregone conclusion. If no system owners were defined, approvals would not have been possible. If there were no evidence of companywide communication of access policies for new systems, requests for access authorization would not have been created consistently. In this environment, the recommendation on periodic access reviews merely sidesteps underlying control fissures.

Even when it comes to the actual implementation of the aforementioned recommendation, other complexities await. For some systems, running an access report on application functions mapped to roles requires further customization or enhancement. Until this is available, an excessive amount of time has to be spent manually assembling the access report through a combination of varied system inputs and screenshots. The auditor as Observer is disinterested in none of these practical constraints; displaying neither patience nor aptitude for wading through uncertainty, she is but a shadow that appears on the horizon, waves a finger and proclaims get it done or else. She does not care how the finding is remediated; merely that it is, oblivious to the amount of work and rework, or bloodbath, behind the scenes.

On the opposite end of the spectrum, the auditor seized by the Authoritarian archetype dictates the remediation to undertake and sees her way as the *only* way. "Can't you see the importance of this?" "We need to have this implemented ASAP." It does not matter that stakeholders are working together to bridge communication breakdowns on new hires across Human Resources (HR), Engineering, and Accounting functions. All she wants to see is conclusive evidence of management signoff on the dotted line. Auditors dominated by Authoritarian archetypes are resistant to change. When auditees volunteer changes in the control environment that may render specific controls redundant or unnecessary, their instinctive response is to say no. We have a choice when it comes to responding to the cards we have been dealt. We can choose to remain open or we can develop a protective envelope, shielding us from having to entertain what others have to say or do. In the latter approach, we stick to our guns, insisting upon the veracity of our own truths, whilst unaware that our solutions can in turn create their own problems. Shadow archetypes propel one another. The auditor as Critic during audit planning spurs the auditor as Interrogator during fieldwork; the auditor as Interrogator gives rise to the auditor as Authoritarian during issue identification and remediation. Interestingly, had the Skeptic archetype surfaced at this point, the auditor would have been more inquisitive and thus more open to questioning even her own recommendations. The resulting Sleuth archetype would have sought out counterhypotheses and entertained opposing viewpoints. In this manner, the Authoritarian archetype begins to lose its grip.

Whilst the Observer shadow lacks the Protector archetypal energy, and the Authoritarian shadow is inundated with it, both shadow archetypes share an aversion to ambivalence. Where the auditor as Observer does not care to take a dip in the pond of reality, the auditor as Authoritarian overcompensates by diving in, displacing the water, and insisting it has been dry all along. I am reminded of someone whom I used to work with. "Controls are straightforward; either you have them or you don't," he once told me. The auditor as Observer does not care enough; the auditor as Authoritarian cares too much. The former protects her non-involvement; the latter protects her self-involvement. Against these polar opposites, the auditor as Protector protects the interests of her client.

Just what does protection entail specifically? Issuing commandments and watching over remedial efforts is not protection, more like dictatorship. It is this rather oppressive environment that leads many auditees to watch what they say or convene beforehand amongst themselves to figure out a game plan before meeting with the auditor. In this case, the auditor, having played no significant part in developing a solution, is relegated to a mere mouthpiece back to management. To speak of protective measures, one needs to first address just what or who we are protecting ourselves from. The overzealous auditor is likely to allocate inadequate time and resource to this area, or else miss it altogether.

Risk is fast becoming an overused word. If the present plethora of risk certifications is any indication, organizations today are in need of resources to mitigate risk. Yet, most of us mistake risk avoidance for risk mitigation. Simply redesigning the data flow such that the organization does not transmit, process, or store cardholder data is a means of avoiding risks that come with handling sensitive payment information; most service providers choose to employ this means as they do not have in-house capabilities. Risk mitigation is an altogether different discipline, often comprising a combination of preventive and detective means – restricted access, network monitoring, and data encryption – of securing company assets, or in our example, cardholder data. The auditor as Protector works with management to devise primary and secondary safeguards. Specific controls may not be operating effectively, in which case compensating controls would be devised. For instance, until the newly installed network intrusion tool has been properly configured and stress-tested, the auditor as Protector may work with auditees to identify an interim manual review of access logs for suspicious login activity. In some cases, the management view of risks may require a re-orientation. As Michael Gibbins, Susan McCracken, and Steve Salterio point out in their study of auditor–auditee negotiation of accounting issues, client management tends to see the issue identified as a standalone concern, whereas audit partners are inclined to see the issue as a larger set of client specific concerns.[11] Elsewhere, Carnegie Mellon University's Software Engineering Institute (SEI) research on systems thinking and insider threats reveal how risks can co-mingle

---

[11] Michael Gibbins, Susan McCracken and Steve Salterio, "The Auditor's Negotiation Strategy Selection: Nature of the Auditor–Client Management Relationship and Flexibility of Initial Accounting Position", August 2006, *http://ssrn.com/abstract=934383.*

through feedback loops. The auditor's role here is to convince management of risk interdependencies in a holistic context.

To truly serve as a guardian of enterprise security, the auditor needs to build trust. Building trust is more than social networking and camaraderie. From a psychological perspective, she needs to be vigilant of instances where she may project her archetypal shadow on others. For instance, rather than acknowledge the Observer shadow archetype latent within, she perceives auditees as Observers, faulting them for not being as engaged in the discourse on internal controls. Her tone becomes overbearing, her demeanor controlling. The Authoritarian without merely masks the Observer within, ignorant of day-to-day operational fires faced by auditees. From a cognitive perspective, she needs to be wary of "either/or" thinking. Taken to its extreme, she can start to screen out what auditees say after hearing "no we don't have this control, but." A steering committee for major system enhancements may make sense for a multi-billion dollar conglomerate; for a small start-up, it may comprise two members talking at each other until they are blue in the face. Context is key. What often appears irrational at the outset is anything but once we take context into consideration. Just as refugees may take a longer route in fleeing war-torn home countries, often travelling at night and through challenging terrain in order to remain undetected, an organization may take a longer, far more circuitous route to mitigate identified control risks. It may choose to implement an automated purchase requisition application for selected powerusers who submit requisitions in high volumes and are vociferous in voicing their opinions before rolling it out companywide. This way, ongoing tweaks can be made to the system during as well as after go-live and users who initially needed kid gloves are given the opportunity to graduate to system proponents.

For Austrian-born philosopher, Rudolf Steiner, "to explain a thing, to *make it comprehensible*, means nothing other than to place it in the context from which it has been torn by the arrangement of our organization."[12] Otherwise, we are merely sensing, not really relating to the matter at hand. To protect is to embrace the big picture – both good and bad – and figure out a way through the thicket. For the traditional father figure as the Protector, there is a sense of inclusiveness, care and, ultimately, accountability. To escape the confines of the Observer and yet sidestep the travails of the Authoritarian, we need to be conscious of how Aristotelian two-value logic shapes our thinking and behavior. Every time the following words crop up in an audit – pass/fail, yes/no, either/or – therein lies an invitation to recognize how we are influenced by the maxim, "this is either A, or not A." To this, we need to respond by digging deeper, peeling back the layers. Consider the following audit scenario. The client appeared to have controls in place and was perceived to have "passed" the audit. The next year, however, auditors returned to find the specific controls not working. It was determined that the key personnel performing the control had left the organization. Subsequent training of new personnel was conducted and compensating controls were identified with adequate time for remediation testing before year end. Once again, the client prevailed, "passing" the audit. Yet from the perspective of organizational sustainability, has the client

---

[12] Rudolph Steiner, *Intuitive Thinking As A Spiritual Path*, Anthroposopic Press, Hudson, New York (1995).

really "passed" the test? To what extent can controls be relied upon to sustain the organization through change? More pointedly, can entity-wide processes or procedures be relied upon for someone else new to step in and perform the same controls to mitigate risk? Dharma master, Nargarjuna, introduced the idea of four-valued logic in which something can be (a) true, (b) not true, (c) both true and not true, (d) neither true nor not true. In our audit scenario, the client appears to (a) have controls in place, (b) not have controls in place, (c) have controls and no controls in place, (d) have neither controls nor no controls in place. Recurring audit near-misses are often symptoms of deeper foundational issues.

To be an effective Protector, the auditor needs to recognize that there is more than meets the eye. There is an old story of a worker suspected of stealing. Every evening when he leaves the factory, the guards inspect the wheelbarrow he pushes before him and find nothing; what they do not realize is that he is stealing the wheelbarrows themselves. Let's revisit this narrative in the context of recurring audit near-misses. Suppose each quarter, when an access review is performed, suspicious test accounts show up in the production environment of a key financial application. The application administrator explains that these may have been created by the third-party support provider as a means of troubleshooting production bugs that cannot be replicated in the test environment. In any case, the administrator deletes them each time following the system owner's quarterly review. No further investigation is performed by the auditor. The access review control is operating effectively each quarter; for all intents and purposes, the stakeholders "passed" the audit. Whether or not we have truly safeguarded the financial application from unauthorized access remains to be seen. Had the auditor examined the audit log activities of the test accounts, he may uncover significant download activities related to sensitive customer information. In this case, the test accounts constitute the wheelbarrow. But unlike the factory guards who peer intently into the wheelbarrow each time the worker leaves, the auditor is satisfied that the wheelbarrow is disposed of each time. Consider an alternate variant of the same scenario. Suppose personnel from the third-party support provider assert that they did not create the test accounts. A review of help desk tickets also revealed no issues requiring production login as part of bug resolution. In fact, audit logs showed the admin account being used to create the test accounts each time. In this case, the veracity of the administrator's account is placed in question. Let us take this example a step further. Suppose the administrator, when questioned, insists that she did not create the test accounts. Further examination reveals that she has kept the same default administrator password supplied when the software was purchased. This password is also immune from periodic password expiry configured for end-user accounts. In the final third act, any user with knowledge of the default password whether in the client, support, or software provider capacity could be a perpetrator.

We are predisposed to suspect technical personnel who have privileged access to a given system. We are drawn to news involving an abuse of privileged system access. In 2006, for instance, a system administrator employed by UBS PaineWebber planted a logic bomb, intended to cripple about 1,500 networked computers in branch offices around the country, in protest over the bonus he received, ultimately costing his financial services firm more than $3 million to assess and repair the damage. Yet, in the latest study of insider financial fraud conducted by the CERT Insider Threat Center of CMU's SEI, in collaboration with US Secret Service (USSS), nearly 93 percent of the 80 fraud incidents occurring between 2005 and 2012 were committed by someone who did not hold a technical position within the organization or have privileged access to organizational systems.[13]

The what-if and real-life scenarios above underscore the importance of the manner in which the auditor as Protector remains vigilant. Just as boundaries continue to shift or change, the auditor entrusted with the Protector archetype needs to be reminded time and again that the very fences she has helped erect may no longer work, or, worse, be used to abet potential system compromises. By balancing the Protector archetype with its Skeptic and Sleuth counterparts, she feels less compelled to always dispense advice: watch out, do not do this, that will never work. For various reasons, this balance may not be easy to achieve. To assist with control buy-in and implementation, she needs to articulate the risks succinctly, convincingly, to management and key stakeholders. Over time, however, she may never quite relinquish her role as internal advocate or proponent for this very control or, at a minimum, hand it over to company personnel. If she is not careful, she may be imprisoned by the persona of a prison warden or watchdog. So fixated is she on maintaining control, she remains unaware even as the once familiar division begins to recede further into the horizon.

---

[13] Adam Cummings, Todd Lewellen, David McIntire and Andrew P. Moore, "Insider Threat Study: Illicit Cyber Activity Involving Fraud in the U.S. Financial Services Sector", Special Report CMU/SEI-2012-SR-004 (July 2012).

Exercise

Paradoxes confound our assumptions. They make us stop, laugh at ourselves, think, and, in the process, respond more fully to the present. Imagine showing up at your client's facility and hearing the following from your auditee:

- I am lying
- I know nothing
- No negativity please.

Reflect on your audit engagements. Might there be similar paradoxical observations? As an example, see mine:

- No exceptions have been identified in the monitoring control that detects and mitigates risks
- Reporting to the same management, auditors perform their work objectively
- Most IT general computer controls are of a manual nature.

Now for each identified paradox, consider what it means for your role as the Protector:

- In the aftermath of Enron and SOX, we have become so intent on evidencing the performance of a control, we sometimes forget to ask the simplest question. What errors, if any, showed up in a detective review? If no errors or anomalies are found over the course of several years, what purpose does this control serve other than a check-the-box exercise? Is operating effectiveness merely evidenced in the performance of the review or does it really address the actual detection of possible gaps or weaknesses? How effective is the manager performing a detective review? No one understands a process better than someone performing it day in and day out. In this regard, the manager may be portraying a process as how she thinks it is or should be. To effectively safeguard an organization's interests, the auditor as Protector needs to challenge prior assumptions and reassess existing controls periodically in the clear light of day.

- In early 2012, the US Department of Agriculture (USDA) Food Safety and Inspection Service (FSIS) made the front page of *The New York Times* when it proposed shifting the responsibility for inspections from agency inspectors to employees at slaughtering plants. Perhaps a less proverbial example of the fox guarding the chicken coop is the seldom talked about fact of internal auditors reporting to management and providing an independent opinion simultaneously. Whilst it is true that the Institute of Internal Auditors (IIA) recommend that internal auditors report to the Audit Committee of the Board of Directors, daily administrative oversight is typically provided by the CFO or Controller in the absence of a chief audit officer in smaller companies. Or consider how third-party service organizations engage the services of audit firms to put together a SSAE 16 (formerly SAS 70 Type II) report on the health of internal controls. I have yet to see a report that flunked the compliance posture of the service provider client.

As a Protector, the auditor needs to turn her attention from assessing others to her own lot. To what extent can she be biased? If she is, how does this preclude her from identifying real risks?

- Less discerning clients expect a general computer control audit to be accomplished in quick time to the hum of printers churning out access logs with little dialogue thrown in. The reality is, many IT general computer controls – access reviews, approval of change requests, validation of backup, to name a few – continue to be labor rather than system intensive. To focus on systems and usual suspects such as IT personnel can be a red herring for the auditor as Protector. Gaps typically arise in the actual human interfaces with systems rather than in and of systems.

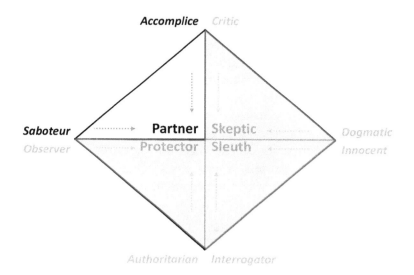

Figure 5: Partner archetype and shadows

Most of us, clients and auditors alike, do not view auditors as partners. When we do, we are more likely to think of audit partners, owners joined by their pooled interest in the audit firm, rather than individuals with whom we can form strong symbiotic relations. In fact, the archetypes covered earlier – Skeptic, Sleuth, and Protector – are more likely used to characterize an auditor. Auditors are often perceived to be a stuffy lot, more at home with sifting and cataloging control paraphernalia than driving any real change or improvement in how things work. Yet, by assessing a process from start to finish, and factoring in the ways things get done, through systematic means or otherwise, an auditor is in a unique position to bridge gaps and build interfaces amongst disparate functions (see Figure 5). The auditor who embodies the spirit of the Partner is a confidant. Folks are not hesitant to seek her counsel. She is approachable yet forthright, fair yet firm, forgiving yet focused. She is typically considered a subject matter expert on internal controls within the organization. Unlike the auditor as Skeptic who brainstorms multiple possibilities, the auditor as Partner is a key asset to execution. Unlike the auditor as Sleuth who may uncover changes long after the fact during a year-end audit, the auditor as Partner is proactively consulted on the risks and options when a new system is implemented or process is changed. Unlike the auditor as Protector who intervenes in the face of emerging risks or aftermath of a security breach, the auditor as Partner serves as a glue to bind everyday operations with compliance, preventing commonplace events or exchanges from going awry.

Just as we do not automatically associate enabling with auditing, we almost always underestimate or take for granted the value of everyday controls. Take, for instance, bumper to bumper traffic and frayed tempers that result from a traffic light outage. In the IT world, imagine what it would be like if the following were an everyday occurrence:

- New system enhancements not only do not work; they also preclude existing functionality from functioning properly, if at all
- Backup that is restored is unusable at best, corrupted at worse

- Updates made in a system can be easily overwritten by another and there is no way of verifying who did what.

As Partners, auditors promote controls that keep our everyday work valid, accurate, complete, and secure. In 2006, the IIA Research Foundation commissioned the IT Process Institute (ITPI) to conduct a study on the impact IT controls have on operational performance. In surveying 330 executives from North American IT organizations, ITPI gathered data on 15 different performance measures including change success rate, incident first fix rate, and repeat audit findings.[14]. Change success rate refers to the percent of changes that were not backed out, did not cause service outage, and were completed on a timely basis. First fix rate pertains to the percent of incidents/outages that were resolved on the first attempt. ITPI was able to segment participants into top, medium, and low performers. Top performers had an average 95 percent change success rate, 12 percent higher than low performers. Higher performers also had a higher first fix rate and lower number of recurring audit findings. ITPI found that IT controls affected large and small organizations differently. What is remarkable is that for the latter group, ITPI found that just three out of 53 IT controls – those pertaining to access control, change management, and error management – predicted 45 percent of the performance variation.

CERT researchers at Carnegie Mellon's SEI approached this from a different perspective, studying how the absence

---

[14] Daniel Phelps and Kurt Mine, *Leveraging IT Controls to Improve IT Operating Performance*, The Institute of Internal Auditors Research Foundation (IIARF), Altamonte Springs, Florida (2008).

of key foundational controls can impact performance.[15] Using system dynamics, they were able to develop a model that explains how, when an IT organization takes shortcuts such as relaxing change documentation and access controls to expedite firefighting to maintain operations, it may see a near-term improvement in system availability by accelerating the problem repair process. However, over the long term, the relaxation of these controls can contribute to unreliable code; the absence of change documentation makes it harder each time to diagnose problems and there is a greater likelihood of unauthorized changes arising from the lack of control.

The consciousness that perceives each thing as existing separately is false ... the more deeply we look ... the more they dissolve[16]

To graduate from the Protector to the Partner archetypes, the auditor needs to come to an understanding of what the great Indian, Mahasiddhi Nargarjuna, terms "dependent arisings." In experiencing our environment as objects and ourselves as subjects, there is an implicit assumption that everything has an independent self-existence. It is this very assumption that Nargarjuna challenges. For, just as a car is dependent on its parts – wheels, engine, seats, dashboard – it has no real existence outside of the materials it is made of or the manner in which we build, use, or assess it against other modes of transportation.

---

[15] Andrew P. Moore and Rohit S. Antao, *Modeling and Analysis of Information Technology Change and Access Controls in the Business Context*, Technical Note CMU/SEI-2006-TN-040 (March 2007).
[16] Dalai Lama, *Essential Teachings*, North Atlantic Books, Berkeley, California (1995).

Consider the following Lao Tzu poem:

Thirty spokes unite at a hub
In their nothingness consists the carriage's effectiveness
One hollows the clay to shape into pots
In its nothingness consists the pot's effectiveness
One cuts doors and windows to make the chamber
In their nothingness makes the chamber's effectiveness[17]

In a sense, internal controls are akin to the hub that unites the spokes of a carriage wheel, the space that accentuates a pot or entrance that secures a chamber. As the ITPI and SEI research can attest, internal controls have far reaching implications for operating performance beyond risk mitigation. So focused are we on the tangible that we forget the space between our cells, in which a third of the water contained in the human body is housed. In a way, this is no different from the disgruntled auditee who sees controls as nothing but superfluous appendages, hindering real work from getting done and contributing to administrative overhead. By dependent arisings, we are not denying the existence of things; rather, we are acknowledging their interconnectedness, the existence of something vis-à-vis others.

Along this train of thought, there is no auditor without auditee, no audit finding without inherent weakness. Gripped by the Protector archetype, the auditor is quick to locate or project evil, guilt, onto others. Recall labels such as hacker, malicious insider, and cybercriminal. According to Jung, this projection "carries the fear which we

---

[17] William P. Coleman, "Tao Te *Ching* – The Classic about Ways And Instances", *http://williampcoleman.wordpress.com/2008/02/07/lao-tzu-chapter-11/* (2008).

involuntarily and secretly feel for our own evil to other side" and consequently "deprives us of the capacity to deal with evil."[18] When it comes to the Partner archetype, we are inclined to shun its shadow archetypes – the Accomplice and Saboteur. By finding them unacceptable, we are unable to see them in ourselves and more likely to project them onto others. The audit becomes a zero-sum game; either we prevail and they lose or vice versa. Take familiar IT audit aphorisms such as password aging and complexity that we take for granted and issue to clients without reservation. Researchers at University College London studied user behavior when it comes to the use of enterprise passwords in two organizations – one with password complexity and aging controls, and other with password aging controls.[19] They found that a disproportionate number of users in the former organization disclosed a fear of forgetting, and went through downtime having helpdesk reset their passwords; consequently many wrote down their passwords. In comparison, none of the users in the latter organization wrote their passwords down. Ironically, the combination of strong password strength and periodic expiry actually led to a more insecure environment where users wrote down passwords. Never mind from a technical perspective, password strength may not be an effective defense against unauthorized access in the first place. Humility and compassion, thus, are key ingredients for overcoming an us-versus-them adversarial auditor–auditee relationship.

---

[18] Carl C. Jung, *Civilization in Translation, The Collected Works of C.G. Jung*, Volume 10, Bollingen Foundation, New York, NY (1964).
[19] Philip Inglesant and M. Angela Sasse, *The True Cost of Unusable Password Policy: Password Use in the Wild*, Department of Computer Science University College London (April 2010).

We experience ourselves, our thoughts and feelings as something separate from the rest ... This delusion is a kind of prison for us – Albert Einstein, 1954

The auditor as Partner widens her lens to look at other metrics beyond traditional audit indicators such as audit findings. Insofar as controls can impact operating performance, other indicators, such as change success rate and first fix rate, come into play. If you look at the lifecycle of compliance management, as new regulations come into play, such as SOX in the initial years, the focus is on remediating control deficiencies. Over time, however, a myopic focus on deficiencies can mask any opportunities to leverage the value of controls in other parts of the enterprise. Process flowcharts developed from internal control work can be used to map operational processes end-to-end to uncover breaks in process. Change management controls for software can be extended to the project level to improve the way the enterprise manages key technology projects.

In embracing the Partner archetype, we become more mindful of the way audits are performed. In adapting system dynamics thinking to audits, we see how, by targeting compliance as an end in and of itself, we risk getting caught in a reactionary loop, recommending quick fixes to address surface symptoms rather than root causes. Attempts to remediate symptoms may burden already stretched resources with additional supervisory oversight or complicate existing control systems with compensating controls. To look beyond symptoms however, we need to ask deeper questions.

- When do lapses typically occur?
- Have they resulted in actual unauthorized activity?

- Have existing controls undercut one another to produce an unexpected outcome?
- Are controls embedded into existing processes or are they an afterthought?
- What do the audit findings add up to?

The story of blind men and the elephant come to mind. When an elephant appeared for the first time in their village, the blind men were intrigued. The first man, who touched its leg, said it was like a pillar. The second, who touched its tail, thought it was like a rope. The third, who touched its ear, said it was a like big fan. And so on. The men began to argue as to who was right. In a way, they were all right, as each felt a different part, all interconnected and making up the elephant, yet they still missed the big picture altogether. To overcome a check-the-box approach to IT audits and compliance, we need to focus on the big picture and interactions rather than dividing it up into individual grid cells. Through this journey, we develop an understanding of the interconnectedness of things.

Take the following risks – delays in time to market, poor access de-provisioning, processing errors, disparate infrastructure – all seemingly unconnected. And yet intuitively is it not likely that in having a hodgepodge of infrastructure with little standardization, it would be difficult to administer user access, let alone disable access for terminated employees in a timely manner? Does it also not follow that, in an environment characterized by disparate infrastructure and access termination difficulties, there would be a higher likelihood of processing errors, what with integrating data from various systems or possible unauthorized access? Finally, faced with all three risks, infrastructure, access, and accuracy, lags in IT responsiveness become all the more likely such as delays in a product launch or release.

George Westerman, a research scientist at the Center for Information Systems Research at MIT's Sloan School of Management, developed an IT Risk Pyramid identifying four enterprise-level risks most affected by IT assets and processes – availability, access, accuracy, and agility.[20] He proposes that risk factors form a hierarchy so that having an abundance of these at the bottom tier – such as having disparate infrastructure, poor patch management, and backup – can not only increase availability risks but also access, accuracy, and agility risks in upper tiers. Conversely, upper tier risks in accuracy and agility can be lowered by first targeting foundational-level risks in availability and access.

From an IT control perspective, we see how IT general computer controls tend to address the bottom tier availability and access risks, whereas application controls tend to address upper tier accuracy risks. Today, much has been written and said about the role of auditors, how we are continually challenged to better assist management in managing risks. And yet, we still have a long way to go in becoming more risk aware. In its report on the first year implementation of Auditing Standard 5 – AS5 was adopted in 2007 with the intent to guide auditors in performing more risk-based, top-down audits in complying with SOX – Public Company Accounting Oversight Board (PCAOB)

---

[20] George Westerman, *IT Risk Management: From IT Necessity to Strategic Business Value*, Center for Information Systems Research Sloan School of Management, Massachusetts Institute of Technology, MA (December 2006).

cited inadequate attention paid to risks arising from deficiencies in IT general controls after reviewing over 250 audits performed by eight of the largest US public accounting firms.[21] To better appreciate the importance of pervasive level risks and associated IT general computer controls, the first step may very well be to gain a deeper insight into how risks interrelate within the organization rather than worry about itemizing risks, a check-the-box-approach.

The Protector archetype is all for boundaries, definitions, and divisions. The Partner archetype, on the other hand, embraces interconnections, dependencies, and wholeness. The auditor as Partner respects silences, spaces, and intermissions between occurrences or events. What is unsaid or swept under the rug is often more telling than what is actively parlayed. Taken to the extreme, however, the auditor as Partner may acquire its shadow, the Accomplice. Audits become no more than nods-and-winks affairs, both parties toeing the corporate line and reaching a consensus on the nature of audit findings to report on each time. "You know auditors, they have to find something," is a typical symptomatic fallout of the Accomplice at work. Another is "give them something to chew on, low-hanging fruit" or "better this finding than a real deep-dive into the Pandora box." On the opposite end of the spectrum, the auditor as Saboteur goes against the current stream of collective efforts. During user prototype testing for a new

---

[21] Public Company Accounting Oversight Board, "Report On The First-Year Implementation of Auditing Standard No. 5, An Audit of Internal Control Over Financial Reporting That Is Integrated with An Audit of Financial Statements", PCAOB Release No. 2009-006 (September 2009).

application, she recommends restricted access precluding users from trying out different features and becoming familiar with new product functionality. In evidencing backup, she insists on old-fashioned review signoffs despite email notifications on backup status and evidence of help desk resolution during failure of backup jobs. The Saboteur does this sometimes unwittingly because she is viewing controls for controls' sake or purely from a risk or security perspective rather than a usability or performance perspective. For the auditor as Saboteur, a simple withholding of critical information can circumvent a natural progression of affairs to further her aims. Whilst knowing too well that efforts have begun in earnest to remediate an internally identified deficiency, she feels nonetheless compelled to paint this issue in exaggerated proportions, an exercise in self-aggrandizement.

Although the former over-identifies with the Partner archetypal energy and the latter is depleted of this very same archetypal energy, both the Accomplice and Saboteur shadows can be counterbalanced with the Skeptic and Sleuth archetypes. The openness to multiple points of view and ensuing investigation into the very heart of the matter can prompt a rethink of an unstinting manner of either going along with management (auditor as Accomplice) or against everyday operational flow (auditor as Saboteur). The key is not to slay the shadow, but to engage it out in the open. Might there be areas that we overlooked? Is an Accomplice archetype merely a veil for conflicted self-doubts over the real value-add of IT audits to enterprise wide objectives? Conversely, are Saboteur archetypal attempts really driven by a deep longing to have a voice in the organization, a seat at the table? By bringing our shadow archetypes into sharp relief, we clarify our relationships with one another, and in doing so, understand the roles we play in the larger organizational context. The Partner archetype, thus, is an invitation to integrate with others, a return to wholeness.

Exercise

As auditors, we are familiar with "what-if" scenarios. What if:

- Manual procedures are not followed
- The approver goes on vacation
- Access is not removed.

The purpose of this exercise is to employ a different set of what-ifs. Instead of applying these to possible risks as we have in the last chapter, we are interested in exploring possible roles here.

Reflect on the value-add of your audit engagements. What have been some of your accomplishments? Typical ones may include:

- Mitigated key risks surrounding new processes or changes in control owners
- Reduced the number of audit findings year after year
- Automated key manual controls and reduced reliance on resource-intensive reviews prone to error.

What if you were a systems manager rather than auditor? What would be some of your likely accomplishments? Try to think of specific examples. A couple I can think of are:

- Better met business needs by making it easier for folks to submit and approve expense reports through a new web-based tool.
- Improved the time it takes to resolve or escalate a support bug or issue logged with Helpdesk.

Now return to the role of the systems auditor. How might your accomplishments take on the same flavor of the system manager's?

- By recommending the enabling of system validity and completeness checks for key fields and setting up delegate approvers, the number of roundtrip clarifications amongst requesters, approvers, and accounting is minimized. Expense reports are easier to submit, review, and approve.
- Having a different set of controls specific to handling emergency fixes frees up the time it takes to resolve a critical bug whilst ensuring appropriate detective reviews and root-cause analyses after problem resolution. In this manner, Helpdesk is better poised to assist with prioritized issues in a targeted manner.

Consider how this second set of audit accomplishments is more pertinent to a Partner archetype, whereas the first set relates more to a Protector archetype. To the extent that everything is interconnected, how might risk, performance, security be interrelated? By continuing to overemphasize risk mitigation and the Protector archetype in the auditor, to what degree are we shortchanging ourselves and downplaying our potential as a true Partner in making a difference to everyday operations?

PART II: TRANSCENDANCE

CHAPTER 5: IN SEARCH OF ESSENCE

Table 1: Archetypal essence

	Skeptic	Sleuth	Protector	Partner
Essence	Openness	Inquiry	Segregation	Connectedness

We started this book by looking for the essence behind various roles that auditors play (see Tables 1 and 2). In undertaking this journey, we covered the Skeptic Sleuth, Protector, and Partner archetypes, yet how close have we come in truly understanding each of these images? Might each in turn yet constitute a form given rise to by an underlying essence, a puppet, as it were, manipulated by an invisible hand?

Table 2: Essence arising part I

	Protector	Skeptic	Sleuth	Partner
Essence	Segregation	Openness	Inquiry	Connectedness

Take openness in a Skeptic archetype. What can give rise to openness? How about its polar opposite: segregation, an insistence on clarity of boundary, right versus wrong, the very attributes of a Protector archetype. Never mind the nature of the program enhancement, all will undergo three levels of approval. Consider an instance where a client has a specific manner of soliciting authorizations for program enhancements. Rather than varying the number of approvals required by priority or impact, all changes are put through three approvals regardless. Rather than take this at face value, the auditor as Skeptic is motivated to inquire into it. Why three approvals and not two or four? When are they obtained in the software development lifecycle? How are they obtained, simultaneously or sequentially? Do all changes require approvals? An openness to explore possible explanations and outcomes predisposes the auditor to inquire: ask questions, collect samples, validate hypotheses. Through inquiry, the auditor assumes the Sleuth archetype. In this manner, the essence that underscores a particular archetype, the Skeptic in this case, gives rise to another essence that manifests the Sleuth archetype. What of our original question: what compels openness through the Skeptic? Ironically, the very implementation of approvals carte blanche dilutes the effectiveness of what the Protector archetype is seeking to safeguard: validity and integrity of enhancements. Inundated by approval requests, stakeholders begin to turn a blind eye, evidencing their review as if checking a box; exceptions start to fall through the cracks. Compelled by the receptivity of the Skeptic archetype and finds of the Sleuth archetype, the connectedness in the Partner archetype emerges to restore balance to composition of controls in change management. Approvals are tailored to the nature of the program enhancement with performance, security, and compliance in mind. In our example, we see dependent origination at work: the Protector giving rise to the Skeptic, giving rise to the Sleuth, giving rise to the Partner.

We started off this chain of events by asking what can give rise to openness. Let's try a different question this time. What can give rise to inquiry?

Table 3: Essence arising part II

	Sleuth	Partner	Skeptic	Protector
Essence	Inquiry	Connectedness	Openness	Segregation

What about a security breach such as the misappropriation of proprietary or sensitive data? The Sleuth archetype kicks into gear. Inquiry is abetted by connectedness, an ability to relate to stakeholders in hearing their side of the story. In this manner, the Partner archetype is close on the heels of the Sleuth archetype. Hearing does not necessarily translate into believing; the openness to multiple points of view brings forth the Skeptic archetype. When it comes to devising internal controls to prevent the breach from recurring, segregation of boundaries is required; the Protector archetype ensures that assets are properly safeguarded. In this scenario, the Sleuth gives rise to the Partner, gives rise to the Skeptic, gives rise to the Protector (see Table 3).

Our two examples demonstrate the fluid interdependence amongst essences and, by association, archetypes. To cling on to any particular archetype is to miss the point. Even within the lifecycle of an audit, specific archetypes can dominate at various stages. During scoping, the Skeptic emerges to ask key questions that encourage stakeholders to re-examine old assumptions. When performing discovery, the Sleuth leaves no stone unturned, gathering information and mapping out processes end-to-end. Come to the validation of internal controls, the Protector steps forward to ensure that the proper preventive or detective controls are in place. The Partner surfaces when working with the client to develop a feasible solution. To clutch, grasp, or hold on to any one particular archetype is to deny our growth at crucial intervals. The clarity of purpose or conviction enjoyed by the auditor as Protector works at a point in time; faced with changing circumstances, unless this gives way to a receptivity to alternate points of view in the Skeptic archetype, she remains stuck. Conversely, when all options have been explored and brought to the table, the auditor as Skeptic needs to don the Protector archetypal armor, lead the charge with institutionalizing the proposed controls. To continue to waver or second-guess is no different from shooting herself in the foot.

As we all can attest, giving up on habits or accustomed manners, let alone archetypes, is easier said than done. To loosen our grip, it may help to recall that our own search for essence, openness in this case, has led us to something far more elusive; segregation giving rise to openness, giving rise to inquiry, giving rise to connectedness. It would appear that openness has no inherent or intrinsic existence, its attributes ascribed to other essences. To hang on to openness is like clasping at air; it eludes us with each grasp. To continue to latch on to the Skeptic archetype, or any other archetype for that matter, can seem ludicrous, archetypes having no inherent existence of their own other than in relation to one another within a specific context. We become no different from the emperor who parades before his subjects in "invisible" clothes. By hanging on to an archetype, we are under the illusion that we are asserting our identities, coming into our own. But because the archetype has no intrinsic existence, our very actions strip us of our individuality, ironically enough. To be an individual is to be indivisible; the origin of individual arises from in (not) and dividuus (divisible). To hold on to an archetype is to hold on to a part of an elephant and insisting, like the blind men, that it is the whole when it is but one of multiple parts.

Jung defined individuation as a process where one becomes aware, discovers multiple parts within the self. Transcendence unifies oppositional tendencies. Consider the shadow, the archetype we tend to deny or repress. As we have seen in the Skeptic archetype, the Dogmatic and Critic shadows can arise. The former represents a deflated Skeptic where the power of possibility is all but solidified into unyielding dogma. The latter represents an inflated Skeptic where the power of persuasion is emphasized, at the cost of appearing snippy. Transcending the polar opposites means facing them head-on, though not in an adversarial way. To try to defeat the Dogmatic is to risk becoming the Critic; to slay the Critic is to risk becoming the Dogmatic. To transcend is to walk the middle path, acknowledging both positive and negative poles, whilst maintaining the openness that characterizes the Skeptic. This is transcendence within an archetype. Then there is transcendence of archetypes, neither craving nor slighting any one, but embracing the multitudinous of a luminous whole.

The problem arises from clasping any one archetype, or combination of archetypes, for our dear lives. I am reminded of an old tale to catch a monkey. Hollow out a coconut shell by cutting a small hole at one end. Make it small enough to preclude a monkey's hand from passing through when it is clenched. Place some peanuts inside the shell and connect it with a cord. The unsuspecting monkey comes along, reaches for the nuts inside the shell and grasps them in its fist. At this precise moment, pull on the cord. By not letting go, choosing peanuts over life, the monkey gets caught.

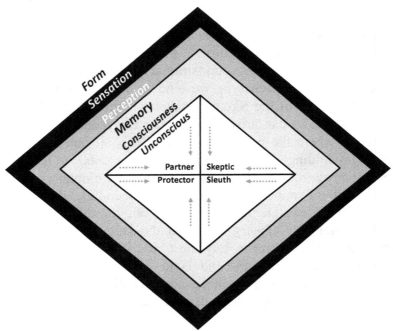

Figure 6: Five skandhas

The Heart Sutra, the essence of Buddha's teaching, describes five ways, or *skandhas* (see Figure 6), a person views the world through:

- Form, *rupa*. Objects appear to us through our sight, sound, taste, smell and feeling
- Sensation, *vendana*. Categorizing and evaluating the objects
- Perception, *sanjna*. The basis for deeming objects positive, negative, or neutral

- Memory, *sanskara*. Assembling experiences and forming habits
- Consciousness, *vijnana*. Developing a knowing of the way we function.

In reviewing the vendor master file, an auditor finds employees set up as vendors. She deems this negative, based on her internal framework. Based on recollections of client fraud arising from employees set up to be paid as vendors, she is able to discriminate what she observes. The Heart Sutra describes the *skandhas* not just as a means by which we see the world but also ways which we carve out our identities. Motivated by what she observes, the auditor takes on the Protector archetype and brings up her findings with the client. The client explains that because there is no separate expense reimbursement tool, the company has set up employees as vendors to cut them checks to reimburse approved expenses. The auditor has various options; she could choose to persist with the Protector archetype and in so doing veer into its Authoritarian shadow. She could allow her Skeptic archetype to surface; investigate actual check disbursements through the Sleuth archetype before working with the client to develop a means to detect any fraudulent payments through the Partner archetype. Whatever her decision, she can, and should, take comfort that an archetype has no inherent existence outside of its context, as we have seen in earlier examples. Rather than hang her identity on any one archetype, she is free to choose. By over-identifying, repressing, or denying any one, she is merely reaffirming its hold over her.

5: In Search of Essence

Form is emptiness, emptiness is form ... The same holds for sensation and perception, memory and consciousness[22]

If, on the other hand, she were to recognize the inherent emptiness within each of the *skandhas* she employs to view the world, the absence of any self-standing existence in each of the archetypes, she would be less inclined to grab at air, as it were. Emptiness does not mean nothingness; by saying that archetypes are inherently nothing, we are not saying they do not exist. Rather, what we are saying is that they coexist vis-à-vis and amongst one another. This is what it means to transcend archetypes. Not to fight or deny them but to recognize their inherent nothingness. If she only knew she were pinning her sense of identity, credibility, or even self-worth on something no less ephemeral than air.

To be open to different archetypes, we need to see through the persona we project to the world. As auditors, we are not known for our sense of humor or charm, more notorious for our calculating approach to risk and caution. As with all jokes, those made at our expense have an element of truth; they point to unyielding aspects of our public persona – auditors who crossed the road because they looked in the prior year's file or those who return to bayonet the wounded after the battle. To transcend our finger-pointing, scapegoating personas, we must first be willing to unclench our fist, release the peanuts back into the coconut shell. A first sign of clinging reveals itself when we bring our public persona home. We are unable to let our guard down, laugh at ourselves, or throw caution to the wind even when it comes to trivial matters. We over-identify with our public

---

[22] Red Pine, *The Heart Sutra*, Counterpoint, Berkeley, CA (2004).

persona. What is public spills into the private. Those of us less willing to part with this persona are less likely to drop an attachment to a specific archetype. Over-identification with a persona can also translate into a denial or suppression of shadow archetypes. We are inclined to find fault or criticize others before they get a chance to see through our personas and into our shadows. We may joke amongst ourselves how controlling client management can be, wit and sarcasm serving as a deflective foil that directs attention away from our own need to control through the Authoritarian archetype or break out of the detached air of an Observer. The more we are invested in maintaining our personas, the less we are in acknowledging our shadow archetypes. They are left to simmer under the surface; quick wit and dry sarcasm dissipate to reveal inner angst and public outburst.

There is no need to struggle to be free; the absence of struggle is in itself freedom [23]

In our quest for certainty, we have doomed ourselves to playing one-dimensional cardboard characters. The Protector archetype, for instance, is useful for dealing with external risks, but over time becomes trying for others, and exhausting for us. In assuming that the Protector archetype we have donned has an inherent, independent, separate existence, we have also unwittingly accorded a separate, inherent, independent existence to the attacker, insider, or cyber thief. They appear intimidating and evil in and of themselves. This level of sheer absolutism easily gives rise to fear and anguish. Rather than see various players as

---

[23] Chogyam Trungpa, *Cutting Through Spiritual Materialism*, Shambhala Publications, Inc., Boston, MA (1973).

interdependent dynamic beings, we engage in a fruitless struggle over boundaries drawn in sand. For Jung, "the self is relatedness." As such, the self, and the selves of others, are malleable. By clutching to a specific image of ourselves and that of others, we are grabbing on to a hollow shell, fearful that it might shatter at any moment. For all our emphasis on securing a sense of self through the five *skandhas*, we are really taking the easy way out, relying on past habits and beliefs rather than entertaining new possibilities for change and transcendence as they present themselves to us. Jeff Moss, who headed up Black Hat and Defcon hacker and security conferences, is a case in point. Before joining the Homeland Security in June 2012, he was a computer hacker known as the Dark Tangent; before this, he worked in the computer security division of Ernst & Young.

When do you let go? Table 4 lists triggering events and behavioral attributes for each archetype. Table 5 lists attributes that are symptomatic of archetypes that have long outstayed their welcome.

Table 4: Archetypal triggers

Archetype	Triggering Event	Triggering Behavior
Skeptic	New process or system Change in personnel	Inquisitive Thoughtful
Sleuth	Fact finding Root-cause analysis	Fact Finding Persistent

Protector	Audit finding	Taking Charge
	Security breach	Assertive
Partner	Client negotiations	Cooperative
	Client buy-in	Building relationship

Table 5: Archetypal fears

Archetype	Outstayed welcome	Fear of
Skeptic	Pessimistic	Uncertainty
	Doubting	
Sleuth	Confrontational	Unreliability
	Suspecting	
Protector	Controlling	Vulnerability
	Righteous	
Partner	Manipulative	Opposition
	Biased	

Take the Skeptic and Partner archetypes. An effective auditor is able to achieve a delicate balance between these two archetypes. Without the former, she is likely to compromise her objectivity and professional opinion; without the latter, she is unlikely to build trust in client relationships. Rather than relying on past habits, she needs to know when to question, when to engage. This start–stop, dynamic nature of the auditor–auditee relationship does not make the auditor appear hypocritical, deceptive, or untrustworthy. Rather, the client learns to trust the auditor precisely because she can expect her to speak up without reservation and yet appreciate the finer nuances in developing a feasible sustainable solution to unify various stakeholders of sometimes competing interests.

Maintaining this balance requires her to respond fully to each moment with the client. She can begin by paying attention to her sensations and perceptions. At what point is she crossing the line from inquisitiveness to pessimism? Consciousness or knowing can come about when she observes her thoughts and behaviors. She may look back at her past client engagements and see a recurring pattern of finger-pointing and mistrust. To break this pattern, she first needs to accept and acknowledge the ways she is limiting her connection to others; rather than seeing others as interrelated beings, she is too paralyzed by doubt and ambivalence to attain any true progress. Might an emphasis on absolute certainty or a lack of faith in human relations be an underlying fear? The more she puts pressure on herself to either deal with or escape from the uncertainty and insecurity, the more she becomes distressed, defensive, and angry. It is a vicious cycle. As John Daido Loori points out, "fearlessness is not just a matter of being without fear; it is a matter of transcending fear."[24]

To become aware is the first step. Awareness opens up one's receptivity to different senses and perceptions. A client's opinion becomes less an attempt at concealment and subterfuge as is a genuine desire to put in place real change and make a difference. Awareness leads to

---

[24] John Daido Loori, *Two Arrows Meeting in Mid-Air: The Zen Koan*, Charles E. Tuttle Company, Inc., Rutland, Vermont (1994), pp. 193–4.

responsiveness. By responding fully to what she is saying or not saying, she starts to let go of her need for certainty. By letting go, she is not giving up. Instead of losing, she is gaining, making room for change, exploring paths not taken.

Responsiveness does not mean confronting or condemning. Rather than attack or circumvent a client's stance on a particular control, the auditor steps out of her doubt, her mind, herself. Responsiveness means acknowledging doubt without identifying with it. Facing, seeing, and watching doubt is like lying on your back and looking at the sky. Much like moving clouds, doubt arises and fades away. There is no need to feed doubt by saying "I should be suspicious because ..." or "I am getting suspicious because ..." Doing so is identifying yourself with doubt. Simply let it go. Another way of responding to doubt is to look for it. Where is doubt? What does it look like? Is it a feeling of uneasiness that is replaced by a different feeling the next minute, and yet another? Or does doubt dissolve into something else such as fear? Am I doubt? In seeing doubt this way, and realizing its inherent emptiness, its dependency on context and human relations, the auditor becomes less compelled to hang on to it. By relinquishing her hold, she is giving herself and her client the necessary space for a two-way dialogue, for ideas to evolve, free from "oughts" or "shoulds." The Partner archetype emerges in the wake of the Skeptic. Recall Lao Tzu's poem from the last chapter. It is the emptiness within that makes a pot.

5: In Search of Essence

Exercise

Find a quiet place. Sit still and center on your breath. Follow your breath as you breathe in, breathe out.

Say your name. Are you your body or your mind?

What feeling or image comes to mind? Follow this feeling. Is it physical? For instance, do you feel a knot in the stomach? Alternatively, do you feel a lightness in your heart?

Focus on this feeling. Where is it going? Where did it go?

Does a distraction enter the picture? Do you remember about an errand to run or appointment to make?

Go back to the feeling. Is it the same? Is it still as strong?

Go back to you. What comes to mind? Do you still hang on to the same idea of yourself?

- ✓Form. I am my body, I am my mind
- Sensation. My anger, my discomfort
- Perception. Based on my beliefs, my values
- Memory. My experiences, lessons
- Consciousness. My way of thinking, analyzing.

If, like me, when you go through the above exercise, you invariably find yourself preoccupied with your sensations, perceptions, and memories, to what extent are your behaviors and reactions triggered by your moods and feelings? When you see a rope in the dark, do you mistake it for a snake?

Try a different exercise. This time recall an event that made you angry. The client could have been late in supplying the requested audit evidence despite your countless reminders. Or you may find yourself circling back to an annoying audit finding with client management year after year despite "securing" consensus on remediation measures the last time round.

First notice your sensations. Do you feel an ache? Is your stomach in knots? Are your shoulders crunched?

Feel the arising emotions. How could they? Impossible! Unbelievable!

Notice the stories that justify these emotions. Who is to blame? If I had known. If only they took the time. If only they were responsible enough.

Ask yourself what you are afraid of in how things might turn out. Would you appear incompetent? Are you going to be blamed? Would you have lost credibility?

Now ask yourself, are you the physical ache? Are you the wave of enveloping anger? Are you the justification or rationale? Are you the scapegoat?

The closer you look, this "you" identity is nowhere to be found.

CHAPTER 6: SHADOW-WORK

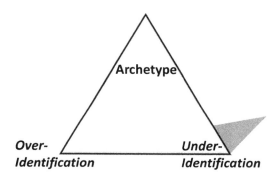

Figure 7: Archetype identification

As auditors, we often find ourselves in circumstances that are different, confounding the very best practices or checklists at our fingertips.

- Employees should not be set up as vendors in the system, yet there were no other means of reimbursing expenses.
- Backups have been configured to run nightly, but the recent slew of notification emails revealed failures over the course of multiple days.
- A newly implemented intrusion detection tool has been disabled due to an overwhelming number of false negatives.
- An augmented round of approvals has yet to preclude errors from arising in submitted transactions.

When tested, we take on archetypal responses. Rather than react unconsciously to the presented challenge at hand, do we take a step back and question underlying assumptions embodying the Skeptic archetype? What exactly has been reviewed as part of an approval process? Do we launch headlong into investigations, leaving no stone unturned as part of the Sleuth archetype? On which days did the backups fail? Was there a recent change to the backup software? Are our shields immediately raised with the Protector archetype? What compensating controls can be put in place until the intrusion detection tool has been fully tested in a sandbox environment? Do we reach out to understand stakeholder needs through the Partner archetype? Is it labor intensive to maintain separate employee records in HR and employees set up as vendors in the financial database? Are there online expense reimbursement solutions we can employ? Can we disable access for terminated employees for processing pending reimbursements before removing them from the system?

At various points, different archetypes may surface only to return at later point in time. This is characteristic of shadow archetypes, images of ourselves that we see as negative (see Figure 7). We deal with our shadows in one of two ways. We may deny them by projecting them onto others, casting them as the enemy. We may suppress them as they resurface time and again. We fight them without realizing that they grow stronger as battle lines are drawn tighter. Yet, as Jung points out, human growth comes from owning our shadows. This is not so much taking control as it is taking notice: acknowledgement; acceptance; letting go. Consider a scenario in which you work with an auditor who appears to get along a little too well with auditees. You suspect her objectivity is compromised and doubt her integrity. Rather than react unconsciously to her manifestation of the Accomplice shadow archetype, find out what makes him get along so well with others. Are there specific attributes that you can relate to, or find yourself envious of? You may see yourself as an objective auditor, but look harder. Are there areas that you are harboring the Accomplice? Do you tend to overlook the omissions or mistakes made by members of your own audit team? To what extent do you "get along" with management better than its reporting personnel? Alternatively, when working alongside the Accomplice, do you play the Saboteur, the foil to her antics? Can her calculating manner in effect bring out your potential as a Partner? Instead of rejecting her altogether, can you tap into your shadow to become whole?

If, on the other hand, you shun the auditor for manifesting the Saboteur, ask yourself: to what extent do you harbor self-sabotaging thoughts? To what extent is your aversion to him really an aversion to your own propensities for sabotaging yourself? When you come to terms with who you are and what you truly deserve, you stop sabotaging yourself. When you stop sabotaging yourself, you can cease blaming him for manifesting the very quality that you fear.

The very shadow elements we fear or despise are useful for turning straw into gold, poison into medicine. As Jung puts it, "we are always discovering new about ourselves ... it is still in the shadow."[25].The Critic's discriminating outlook can be harnessed to push for change in the Partner. Likewise, the Observer's stance can be useful in carrying highly sensitive investigations as a Sleuth. The key is to recognize these shadow archetypes within us and acknowledge their hidden potential. Acceptance is harder

---

[25] C. G. Jung, *Analytical Psychology: Its Theory and Practice*, Pantheon Books, New York (1968), p. 22.

than it sounds. When working with a peer who appears overly susceptible to entertaining varying opinions, thus embodying the Innocent shadow archetype, my instinctual response was to reject him in my mind's eye. Later, much later, after days of using him as a scapegoat for every implementation delay that arose from yet another roundtable discussion on alternatives, I began to explore how I had been unsure, deliberating in my own way. Rather than keeping the communication channel open as he had, my response was to run circles in my mind, combing through each option with a fine comb and hesitating to act. Avoidance, impatience, rage – call it what you will – these are but a myriad of ways we use to avoid facing our shadow. To avoid dealing with my shadow, I blamed him. Acceptance is hard because true acceptance means more than simple acknowledgment, a brief meet and greet. A deeper level of acceptance comes with embracing your shadow. This means admitting to yourself in no uncertain terms you are precisely that you wish to flee. You may be tempted to seek other distractions to avoid the inevitable. For me, accepting parts of myself that were archetypally Innocent went against the very beliefs I held dear. Ruthless execution, timely deliverables, quality work were all that I advocated and strove towards, so reconciling parts of myself that not only slowed the process down, but actively conspired against it in the background, was a significant blow to the ego. But unless I accepted my shadow, there was nothing to let go of.

When it comes to letting go, it helps to balance your shadow against compensating elements. The Critic needs to be periodically reinforced about the value of human faith and virtue – the client attempting to voice her opinion may really be trying, in her own way, to lead her to the real causes – to advocate real improvements as a Partner. The Observer needs to be compelled by a need to feel invested and part of the group to want to hunt down every lead as a Sleuth. From exploring the inherent emptiness of archetypes in the previous chapter, we learn that not much is gained from clinging on to a specific or specific group of archetype. If anything, this puts one at a severe disadvantage, obstinate in outlook and unresponsive to change. It is also a ludicrous proposition, no different from asking someone to clutch at air. Along with this absence of rationale or basis for persisting with an archetype, it also helps to see ourselves as multitudinous creatures not limited to any one or subset of archetypes. Archetypes do not have standalone identities and are submerged or surfaced in relation to others.

Chuang Tzu was an influential Chinese philosopher who lived around the fourth century BCE during the Warring States Period. A well-known Chuang Tzu tale was his dream of a butterfly. "But he didn't know if he was Chuang Tzu who had dreamt he was a butterfly, or a butterfly dreaming he was Chuang Tzu."[26] This anecdote illustrates the interchangeability of identities, in this case between Chuang Tzu and the butterfly. In our context, this can be seen in the interdependent arising's of various archetypes. It also reveals limited awareness, either of Chuang Tzu dreaming about being a butterfly, or a butterfly dreaming about being Chuang Tzu. Whilst embodying a specific dominant archetype, we wear blinkers almost, seeing or perceiving things in a specific manner. Perhaps, more

---

[26] Burton Watson, *The Complete Works of Chuang Tzu*, Columbia University Press, New York and London (1968).

importantly, it underscores the metamorphosis one undergoes to develop a level of awareness about oneself via another. To assume the role of the Critic is to presume a Dogmatic audience. To challenge something, there needs to be an audience who holds a contrary opinion. Transcendence is not so much about metamorphosing from a caterpillar to a butterfly, or in our context from one archetype to another, as it is about recognizing the intrinsic fluidity of things, or archetypes, the ability to parlay constructive feedback into cooperation (from Critic to Partner) or objectivity into truth seeking (from Observer to Sleuth).

An alchemy of sorts is attained when we are able to recognize and work with our shadow archetypes. Psychotherapist and meditation teacher, Rob Preece, is of the view that shadows "contain the forces that are the manure of transformation."[27] By acknowledging and working with negative aspects that we choose to ignore, we can metamorphose these into their positive counterparts through the fire. In the prior chapter, we covered the primary fear faced by each of the four auditor archetypes. Table 6 illustrates some of these compensating elements we can tap into to compensate each fear. Calling up these elements may be an end-of-day or end-of-week exercise. In reflecting upon your travails, see how you can recognize the light before every shadow.

---

[27] Robert Preece, *The Psychology of Buddhist Tantra*, Snow Lion Publications, New York (November 2006).

Table 6: Archetypal triggers

Archetype	Fear	Shadow	Counterbalance
Skeptic	Uncertainty	Critic	Believe or trust people and processes
		Dogmatic	Receptive to changes or differences in opinion
Sleuth	Unreliability	Interrogator	Recognize limits to objective inquiry
		Innocent	Recognize need for independent corroboration
Protector	Vulnerability	Authoritarian	Entertain differences in approach
		Observer	Vested in group objectives
Partner	Opposition	Accomplice	Dare to sound contrary
		Saboteur	Value constructive feedback

If you find yourself reacting as a Critic or Dogmatic, try to see how this can stem from a fear of uncertainty. The Critic battles uncertainty whereas the Dogmatic avoids it. Fight or flee, both are different ways of dealing with uncertainty yet both share the same underlying fear. Explore how this has become a habitual response for you. Try to let this go. In its place, explore how you can regain trust in the people around you or become more receptive to different opinions. Try to see the people around differently as you go about performing your audit fieldwork. When interviewing auditees, if you find your first instinctual response to be one of disbelief, catch yourself and consider how you may appear just as closed minded to your auditees as they are to you. Take time instead to notice the time they have carved out of their busy schedules to be with you, the audit evidence they have prepared, or attention they have devoted to ensuring the accuracy and validity of audited records.

If you find yourself ensnared by an Interrogator or Innocent shadow archetype, ask yourself: to what extent are you fearful of unreliability? The more unreliable a situation appears to be, the more the auditor as Interrogator intensifies her level of inquisition; the more the auditor as Innocent seeks delusion as an alternative. When you see this habitually recurring behavioral response, acknowledge it: catch yourself if your "bedside" manners become a tad grating, or you are merely recording the "pulse." Then let it go. Explore instead how there can be limits to an inquiry conducted by any one particular auditor with any one particular auditee. Most of us have trouble remembering what we had for lunch yesterday or the day before, to say nothing of recall biases and other mental heuristics we employ on a daily basis to get by. Appreciate how auditees are trying their best to get you the requested information. An "I don't know" auditee response can be less an attempt to avoid the question than it is an honest-to-guts reflection of what truly is.

When in the grip of the Authoritarian or Observer shadow archetypes, feel the heated energy of engagement or dispassionate nonchalance of non-engagement. Ask yourself: what are you afraid might happen? To what extent are you powering up your ammunition or defense as an Authoritarian? Conversely, are you running away from ownership as an Observer? Drop your attachment to either of these temperaments. Try instead to embrace a belief in what others have to say or camaraderie with the overall group. You may have fought for specific controls to remediate audit findings at the cost of alienating specific stakeholders or not taken maintenance into consideration. Rather than see audit findings in and of themselves, are they part of a larger cycle of firefighting and symptom remediation, and if so, are there opportunities to make improvements amongst cross-functional stakeholders within the organization?

The Accomplice and Saboteur shadow archetypes can be beguiling. In both, you find yourself actively involved albeit in a diametrically opposite fashion. Question your stance. To what extent are you motivated by a fear of opposition? The auditor as Accomplice silences this further by cozying up with the auditee; although the Saboteur does not deal with opposition upfront, her actions reveal otherwise behind the scenes. Acknowledge these shadow archetypes. Then drop your attachment to them. How differently would events have turned out if you had sought out differences in opinion beyond group-think? If you find yourself seduced by Accomplice or Saboteur shadow archetypes, taking sides without basis, consider for an instant how fortunate you are to be able to view business or system processes end-to-end companywide from interviewing stakeholders across functions. In contrast, entrenched views held by specific constituents may very well arise from a limited lens applied on reality. As an auditor, you are in a privileged position to become a catalyst for enterprisewide change.

Thesis, antithesis, synthesis – Hegel

Jung sees the transcendental "not as denoting a metaphysical quality but merely a transition from one attitude to another. The raw material shaped by thesis and antithesis, and in the shaping of which the opposites are united."[28] The path to transcendence is not a straight line to a fixed goal. Rather, it is more like a spiral trajectory when we are forced to revisit our initial assumptions and solutions, drop attachments to preconceived notions, and continue on a different arc. Each time, we find ourselves trying on different archetypal combinations, relinquishing those that may have worked at one point but have since outlasted their useful lives, becoming receptive to others that may be pertinent to the present set of operating circumstances. The process of piecing something together, deconstructing it, and finally integrating what appears to be disparate elements is a cycle that we undergo time and again as part of our collective and individual growth. At times this feels like an uphill climb; it is far easier to give in to the whims of one's perceived personality, to run on auto pilot rather than remain vigilant to life's possibilities. The more invested we are in clinging onto one-sided stances, the more susceptible we become to the influence of shadow archetypes. What we cannot face within ourselves we will be forced to confront time and again in the external world. Alternatively, we can choose to view each challenge as it presents itself as an opportunity for us to get in touch with

---

[28] C. G. Jung, *Psychological Types*, Princeton University Press, Princeton (1971), p. 480.

underlying vulnerabilities such as fears over not appearing credible or merely performing a check-the-box function. Rather than immediately identify ourselves with our perceptions and emotions, we can choose to view them with curiosity and playfulness. What if we view the same circumstance differently, that is, put in a different lens in the slide projector? Each time we do this, we see changes in the way we view others in relation to ourselves, ourselves in relation to others. Rather than flee our shadow aspects or emulate any one particular archetype, we start to embrace a richer, more complex whole, stepping out of our shadows and into the light.

Of all the archetypes presented, the Sleuth archetypal energy is especially potent for inquiring into the very nature of our mind, our hidden personalities and public personas. Ironically, the desire to free ourselves from our shadow can create its own conditioning pattern. Used to prevail over risks, the Protector archetypal energy may not be appropriate for working with our shadow. Jung points out that "if one side succeeds in winning over ... the process of division will be repeated later at a higher plane" (ibid.). When seeking to prevail over the Critic, you may end up being a Dogmatic. Similarly, whilst seeking to prevail over the Accomplice, you become a Saboteur. By facing our shadow, we are not prevailing over it. Rather, we are choosing to put aside outcome to understand what makes us tick. Through our inquiry, freedom from our shadow becomes a by-product.

Where there is light, there must be shadow, and where there is shadow there must be light[29]

---

[29] Haruki Murakami, *1Q84*, Knopf, Tokyo (2011).

6: Shadow-Work

Ever notice that on some days, you feel like you are on top of the world: your clients are happy with your work, you deliver meaningful findings, and you feel like you have found your calling in life. On other days, you feel sluggish, underappreciated, and overworked. Clients doubt what you say or do, you feel like you are merely checking the box, and nothing seems to pan out right. Most of us go about life fluctuating from one extreme to another. Such is life, we decry, flailing our hands in resignation. Yet, if we were to examine ourselves deeply, we would realize that we carry in each of us the opposite of every virtue that we seek to realize; there is no shadow without light. Conversely, behind every strength or ability lies its negation; there is no light without shadow.

Seen from this perspective, life becomes much less a series of trials and tribulations between good and bad. It is up to us to use our shadow archetype to realize the other. Rather than identify myself immediately with an arising shadow, I have found it useful to name it when it arises. Instead of saying, I feel that what the client is saying is ridiculous, I reframe it by saying the Critic feels that what she is saying is ridiculous. By putting some distance between myself and my reactionary pattern, I feel less compelled to identify with it. There is less of a need to be the aggressor, less impetus for playing the victim. The Critic can be the aggressor. Ask yourself: what is the Critic trying to gain, what is the Critic trying to oppose? Is the Critic trying to appear knowledgeable? Ask yourself: what is the Critic afraid may happen, the outcome the Critic is seeking to avoid? Is the Critic afraid of appearing wrong?

See your shadow archetype as a friend rather than enemy. What is the Critic trying to tell me? What do the Critic's actions reveal? A useful technique I have found for facing my shadow is to amplify it. When I sense myself entrapped by the Critic shadow, I "play" with it during self-reflection. I amplify the Critic's harsh tone, embellish its image with menacing features, and imagine the sheer horror on the faces of the critiqued. For me to come to terms with my shadow, I have found that when I deliberately exaggerate its every gesture in my mind's eye, it becomes easier for me to see through its sheer absurdity. When I get to the point when I do not know whether to laugh or cry, I'm able to drop my attachment to outcome and come face to face with underlying fears.

Another way to see through the shadow's farce is to observe how your behavior changes in relation to others. Do you ever wonder about how the role you acquire changes depending on the person you are with at any given moment? For me, I have noticed that, in the presence of a discriminating, even harsh, Critic, I tend to compensate by being more magnanimous, more receptive to contrary opinions. I am much less likely to identify with the Critic archetype. Instead, I say to myself: hang on, wait a minute, let's hear the client's side of the story. The outcome the Critic is seeking to avoid is not mine. The aggressor role that the Critic is taking on is not mine. It is enough that there is already one Critic, we both do not have to be Critics. Seeing the Critic in this manner helps steer me back to the middle path, embrace the Skeptic archetype between the Critic and Dogmatic opposing poles. I experience not only an external sense of openness to hearing what the client has to say, I also experience an internal sense of openness to the possible archetypes available to me. Like all interdependent phenomena, the Critic arises and fades. Like Chuang Tzu's butterfly fluttering in and out of varied flora and fauna, I can experiment with different roles over time, rather than stay bound to any singular one. It goes without saying that this exercise is easier said than done. Often, I find myself identifying with the Critic shadow for a full day before realizing what I have done. Yet, with patience and practice, you will find that you become better at catching yourself each time. When weariness builds up over the course of an entire day, one's initial tendency is to suppress it by seeking distractions or indulging in it to no end. Yet, it is by undergoing this exercise each time that I feel a true sense of relief wash over me.

Exercise

Look back at your audit engagements and bring up challenging client situations. The client may have been vociferous in opposing remarks. The level of uncertainty or degree of change in the client's environment may have been daunting. Think back to your responses. Name the shadow archetypes that came into play:

- The Critic: What she is saying is ridiculous
- The Dogmatic: Her opinion does not matter
- The Interrogator: She is lying
- The Innocent: She does not make sense
- The Authoritarian: Her actions need more oversight
- The Observer: It is her process
- The Accomplice: She knows best
- The Saboteur: She needs to be taught a lesson.

For each named shadow archetype, ask yourself:

- What is it trying to gain? What is it trying to oppose?
- What is it afraid might happen? What is it seeking to avoid?
- What is it trying to tell you? What is the other? If it is the shadow, what is the light?

For most of us who live in light-infused cities, we cannot see the stars in the night sky. Too much light means the stars are out of sight. To what extent does the awareness of your shadow bring out your light?

CHAPTER 7: INTEGRATING INDIVIDUAL AND COLLECTIVE

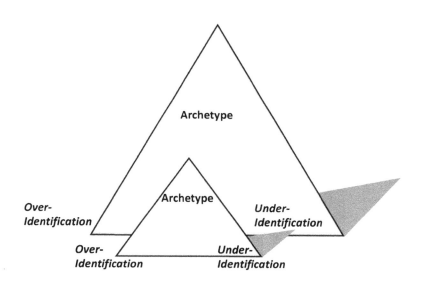

Figure 8: Collective archetype

In working with archetypes and their shadows, it can be easy to personalize specific archetypes. Yet, as Jung points out, archetypes are located in the collective unconscious, where experiences shared by humankind are collected and organized in a similar way. There is also a larger shadow at hand: the collective shadow (see Figure 8). Professor of Comparative Literature, Steve Walker, remarks on how the collective shadow rears its head when we project our collective shadow onto another group, political party, or nation.[30] Originating in the late nineteenth century, the Yellow Peril was used to characterize the threat to Western living standards and culture posed by the influx of Eastern Asian laborers willing to work for low wages. Conversely, the foreign devil, Gwai Lo, or white ghost, was used by the Chinese to characterize European sailors when they arrived in Southern China in the sixteenth century. In the IT audit and security arena, the collective shadow can be seen in the labels we employ to characterize the opposing other: cybercriminal, cyber underground, and malicious insider. When auditors, as a group, are convinced of their own moral goodness and self-righteousness, the collective shadow is lurking. Invariably, they project this shadow onto the other group, casting the other as untrustworthy, irresponsible, or unethical. This is aided in no small part by the media that sensationalizes events to scintillate the masses. Bankers are seen to be motivated by greed and profit-making. Hackers are perceived to be irresponsible, attention-seeking individuals spurred by the prospect of thwarting day-to-day operations. Yet, when examined by their governing body, the PCAOB routinely finds instances when auditors' objectivity has been compromised in long-standing relationships with audit clients and the pressure to sustain a consistent audit income stream.

Every now and then, we end up with egg on our faces, depending on which way the wind blows. In November 2011, auditor watchdog, Francine McKenna, posted a piece at Forbes called "99 Problems and Auditor PwC Warned about None," chronicling how PricewaterhouseCoopers

---

[30] Steven F. Walker, *Jung and the Jungians on Myth*, Routledge, New York and London (January 2002).

gave the bankrupt brokerage MF Global – which commingled its own money with customer accounts – a clean report as recently as May and billed MF Global $12 million for its services over the last year.[31] Retired Ernst & Young Global vice chairman, and presently Silicon Valley Bank chairman, Roger Dunbar, told the PCAOB, at a recent forum on auditor rotation, "I am personally worried about audit firms trying to get you to spend money with them on consulting. It's a risk."[32] In 2012, auditors of Under Armour, a Baltimore-based sports apparel company, lost in the postal mail an unencrypted flash drive containing names and social security numbers belonging to 5,400 employees worldwide.[33]

Rather than acknowledge our own collective shadow when it comes to negligence, we unconsciously project it onto others. The projection becomes all too real when we hear auditees openly acknowledge their omissions when confronted. I remembered being part of a task force responsible for restoring a corrupted database. During root-cause analysis, there was a lot of finger pointing and speculating. Who did this? How could they be so inconsiderate? What were they thinking? Why would they

---

[31] Francine McKenna, "99 Problems and Auditor PwC Warned about None", *Forbes* (October 2011), http://www.forbes.com/sites/ francinemckenna/2011/10/31/mf-global-99-problems-and-auditor-pwc-warned-about-none/.

[32] Francine McKenna, "Auditors Are Asleep at the Switch on Banks' Risk Controls", *American Banker* (July 2012), http://www.americanbanker. com/bankthink/auditors-asleep-at-switch-on-risk-controls-1050923-1.html.

[33] "Under Armour Employees' Personal Information Lost", *CBS Baltimore News*, April 2012, http://baltimore.cbslocal.com/2012/04/21/ under-armour-employees-personal-information-lost/.

put us through this? When the key culprits were identified and questioned, all of them expressed that they had no idea that each of their omissions amassed to a conflagration of errors fanned by an overall absence of companywide policies. When we project undesirable aspects of our group onto another, we actively conspire to diminish our own power. We advocate equality, decry injustice, rally against conformance yet, unbeknownst to us, we hold the very key to unlock our freedom. The other that we so actively oppose is but a projection of our own collective shadow. It becomes an almost cruel irony of sorts when we realize that us-versus-them is really us-versus-us.

To understand our relationship to the larger collective, consider how a hologram is produced. The object is first bathed in the light of a laser beam. A second laser beam is bounced off the reflected light of the first culminating in a swirl of dark and light lines captured on film. When the film is illuminated by yet a third laser beam, a three dimensional object appears. When a hologram is sliced up, each part displays a smaller image of the whole; each snippet thus contains all the information possessed by the whole. In 1982, physicist, Alan Aspect, and his team discovered that, regardless of distance, subatomic particles such as electrons instantaneously communicated with each other. This violated Einstein's long-held tenet that no communication can travel faster than the speed of light. In explaining this phenomenon, physicist, David Bohm, described an aquarium containing a fish filmed by two television cameras, one directed at the front and the other directed at the side.[34] By watching through the two television monitors, it would be plausible to assume two rather than one fish; yet, when one turns, the other moves too. Under these circumstances, a likely conclusion is that the fish are communicating with each other, when they are really part of a whole. This one-in-all, all-in-one phenomenon is also described in Asian philosophies. In Chuang Tzu's butterfly narrative, both he and the butterfly are dreaming; one is within the other. Two different perspectives, each referring to the other, make up a whole. In the net of Indra, a metaphor from Mahayana Buddhism, each "eye" of the net is a jewel which reflects all other jewels, and is reflected in all other jewels. In the Tang dynasty, Buddhist sage, Fa Tsang, led Empress Wu to a room lined with mirrors on its walls, ceiling, and floor. In the middle, he placed a Buddha statue. With a crystal in his hand, he demonstrated how each image of the Buddha reflected from the mirrors was contained in the crystal and reflected back into the mirrors. This mirroring effect can be seen in synchronicity. You know those times when you decide to veer away from the script – your checklists or practice aides – guided by a gut instinct and, hey presto, uncover a fortuitous find? I myself encountered instances when I instinctively asked for a help desk log of issues reported only to uncover the very reasons behind backend database changes.

From a different perspective, authors Connie Zweig and Steve Wolf point out that the personal shadow "is shaped by a confluence of forces: the collective or cultural shadow,

---

[34] David Bohm, *Wholeness and the Implicate Order*, Routledge, London (1980).

which forms the sea of moral and social values in which we swim."[35] Our predilections or inclinations are far more conditioned by those around us than we would like to acknowledge; it is this very reason that certain auditor archetypes thrive in some environments yet languish in others. In his book, *A Little Book on the Human Shadow*, the poet, Robert Bly, distinguished between the personal shadow, the town shadow, and the national shadow.[36] In the chapter, "The Long Bag We Drag Behind Us," Bly describes how, over time, we stuff parts of our being that parents, school, or society dislike into a long invisible bag that we drag behind us. As external auditors, you may encounter internal auditors in specific organizations dominated by Protector and Sleuth archetypes. Unbeknownst even to themselves, they reflect larger archetypal patterns of the overall organization like jewels in Indra's net or the mirrors in Empress Wu's room. This is the assumption we implicitly consent to behind every commonly espoused management practice such as top-down corporate tone, culture, and values. As Jung put it, "on close examination, one is always astonished to see how much of our so-called individual psychology is really collective."[37]

---

[35] Connie Zweig and Steve Wolf, *Romancing the Shadow: A Guide to Soul Work for a Vital, Authentic Life*, Wellspring/Ballantine, New York and Toronto (February 1999), p.17.

[36] Robert Bly, *A Little Book on the Human Shadow*, HarperOne, Australia (June 1988).

[37] Carl C. Jung, *Two Essays on Analytical Psychology, The Collected Works of C. G. Jung*, Volume 7, Bollingen Foundation, New York, NY, (1966), Second Edition, p.155.

The concepts of inherent emptiness and dependent arising we discussed in the prior chapters underscore the interconnected reality we live in. This does not mean what we do is unimportant; on the contrary, what we do, or what identities we claim, becomes one of supreme importance, because it affects everything we are connected to, just as everything in turn affects our very being. Just as our archetypal responses are triggered by what others around us say or do not say, do or do not do, the repercussions of our perceptions, intentions, or actions have implications more far reaching than we realize. Visualize each archetype as a lens in a slide projector. Specific archetypal attributes, when illuminated, are projected on the organizational canvas upon which we conduct our affairs. Just as the archetypes we embody are dependent on the myriad of interweaving organizational threads (all-in-one), we each have the potential to tug at, pull, or manipulate them (one-in-all). The cusp of transcendence lies in realizing the possibilities we have in influencing others, and the varied ways their responses can in turn elicit specific attributes, bringing the full force of specific archetypes to bear.

In organizations with an overbearing almost autocratic tone, it may be easy for auditors within to overlook their ability to provide necessary compensating elements, if only to provide a fresh, new way of looking at or handling the same thing. In lieu of auditors as Sleuths or Protectors performing scheduled year after year compliance audits, such organizations are better served by auditors as Skeptics or Partners who are capable of introducing or fostering much needed change in business processes or system implementation reviews. The one-in-all phenomenon seen in a spliced fragment of a hologram is not intended to over-inflate our sense of self or engorge our already entrenched archetypal personalities. Rather, it speaks to the varied elements in others that we see or reflect in ourselves. When possessed by a Protector archetype for instance, we are likely to emphasize boundaries between ourselves and others, an us-versus-them mentality, one that we can transcend partly by realizing that, in spite of our individual stances on specific matters, we share common behavioral patterns. Letting go of a Protector archetype may, in effect, translate into a series of meticulous endeavors focused on removing the archetypal slides accumulated over time. Conditioned by how we see ourselves and others, through the five *skandhas*, the slide collection gives us an illusion of self that we cling to. As Jung put it, "the ego is like a moving frame on a film."[38]

By daring to break with convention, the auditor is able to provide unique value-add by transcending her ascribed archetype within the organization. This is not to be confused with attempts to gain personal recognition. Our "faculty of imitation," as Jung terms it, can easily lead us on a search for grandiosity: we model ourselves after specific individuals who stand out from the crowd. In audit conferences, it is not uncommon to find folks imbued with self-pomposity, declaring themselves governance evangelists or control champions. You can find them expounding their latest finds before lunchtime conference attendees amidst the clinking of glasses and flatware. Transcendence of archetypes is not about making oneself stand out. Ironically, by doing so, one unconsciously chains one's identity to that of the organization so that if the

---

[38] C. G. Jung, *Analytical Psychology: Its Theory and Practice*, Pantheon Books, New York (1968), p. 22.

latter's stance were A, one invariably feels compelled to espouse B to make a point. It is a tiring if not fruitless pursuit with one forever playing catch-up to the dominant ideology at hand, transcendence for transcendence's sake rather than culminate in any real gain for the client organization. True transcendence realizes the interdependent nature amongst the archetypes held by the auditor and those held by the people around him, in the same organizational context. Unique value-add is furnished when the auditor is able to provide the requisite counterfoil to prevailing thought patterns so as to present a fuller, more complete picture of reality that can, in turn, be used to make informed decisions. During the rollout of a procurement tool, rather than subscribe to the prevailing management opinion that designated approvers are not taking the time to review purchase requisitions in a responsible manner – approving them carte blanche in the system – the auditor, upon closer inspection and independent corroboration, uncovers that most approvers do not even know their departmental budgets in the first place. How then can they be expected to make informed choices when it comes to approving or rejecting purchase requisitions? The solution lies not in improving system adoption, but in clarifying and communicating procurement policies. In this instance, by tapping into a combination of Skeptic and Partner archetypes, the auditor is able to challenge management's stance and provide greater insight into the inner workings of the organization. Seen in this manner, an organization with a different archetypal makeup from that of the individual auditor can encourage her to stretch her limits, draw out her potential.

If you are responsible for hiring or assigning audit personnel to make up a team or group, it helps to see the interplay of individual and collective archetypes. To the extent that teams sharing the same dominant collective archetype also share the same collective shadow, they are unlikely to evolve over time or adapt to take on other archetypes. Whilst these teams may be quick to act or think as one, dominating ideologies, as well as voluntary or involuntary exits of team members exhibiting incompatible archetypes, can all contribute to a stale stasis of sorts. In contrast, whilst a diversity of archetypal manifestations within the same team can slow down the decision-making process, such as increased face time when obtaining consensus on the right course of action, it can also serve to balance out any over or under identifications of specific archetypal energies. Just as a management team focused singularly on profits at the exclusion of social accountability and compliance is likely to run the company amok, an audit team focused singularly on partnering with clients at the cost of objectivity and professional ethics is likely to become a fox guarding the henhouse. On the other hand, a constant cycle of Hegel's "thesis, antithesis and synthesis" amongst different members of the same audit or project team can provide the necessary archetypal balance to attain real progress. This is not to be mistaken as favoring the whims of one or several over the collective good. Our history is a testament to the sheer violence and horror that can result from any one dominant ideology and belief. Against this backdrop, a distribution of myriad archetypes may indeed be necessary in preventing a collective pursuit of extremities with unrelenting velocity.

Just as the auditor is a multidimensional being capable of drawing upon a multiple of archetypes at any given point, she must too recognize this faculty in others. Rather than view them idealistically as one-dimensional carbon copy constructs of good or bad, based on their compliance or lack thereof with accorded controls and procedures, she is better served by understanding the principle of polarity: positive and negative are but different aspects of the same system. To rid one of the other is to attempt to uproot the entire system. The art to devising controls lies in keeping these polar opposites in check. How can we incent sales personnel to sell more products yet rein in their ability to make significant changes to established price schedules? How can we accord more accountability to department heads to manage their respective expenses whilst ensuring that all purchases are valid and authorized? The cyclical nature of good versus bad is illustrated by the Taoist story of an old farmer who had worked his crops for many years. One day his horse ran away. Upon hearing the news, his neighbors came to visit. "Such bad luck," they said sympathetically. "Maybe," the farmer replied. The next morning the horse returned, bringing with it three other wild horses. "How wonderful," the neighbors exclaimed. "Maybe," replied the old man. The following day, when attempting to ride one of the wild horses, his son was thrown and broke his leg. The neighbors again came to offer their sympathy on his misfortune. "Maybe," answered the farmer. The day after, military officials came to the village to draft young men into the army. Seeing that the son's leg was broken, they passed him by. The neighbors congratulated the farmer on how well things had turned out. "Maybe," said the farmer. In our procurement example, procurement policies on budget definitions and approval thresholds are clarified and communicated companywide. Purchases through the procurement tool are put through an appropriate level of review and oversight. The auditor as Sleuth and Partner rejoices. Over time, however, the number of requisitions put through the system declines; yet company expenses continue to rise. The auditor as Sleuth and Protector investigates the situation and uncovers a disproportionate level of expenses being submitted as expense reimbursements rather than purchase requisitions. Because expenses are submitted after they are incurred, and in some cases with considerable time lag, the company runs the risk of failing to accrue for appropriate expenses in a timely manner. It is back to the drawing board to fine-tune company policies to differentiate company purchases from expense reimbursements.

We seek refuge in groups. As external auditors at a client facility, you form deeper connections with your peers than your auditees. As internal auditors, you form specific circles at work, either through team organization or common projects. You are more likely to consult as well as counsel members of your group than you would those in other groups. It helps to see how your group perceives other groups as well as how other groups perceive your own. Because archetypes are relational, they can arise as a result of interacting with other groups. In a pre-implementation system review, participating auditors may be viewed by other groups – project leads, developers, and change management consultants – as gatekeepers who slow down the go-live process. Has access been segregated between development and production? Are corresponding system controls configured to replace manual ones? Is a rollback plan in place for every scheduled phased release? Are process flowcharts and procedure documentation in place to support user adoption during go-live? Certainly, these are necessary audit questions, ones that preclude things from going awry, but certain members of the implementation team may project a Saboteur collective shadow on the auditors' participation. In the midst of resolving bugs encountered in the test environment and responding to late enhancement requests, the internal control considerations can seem like administrative housekeeping. Conversely, the audit team may project an Accomplice collective shadow onto other groups. Certain members may feel that the enhancements are not tested in a complete manner in a rush to meet project milestones or deadlines. Or key intervening controls are sacrificed in an attempt to accelerate cycle times.

Look at your own role in this context. To what extent are you contributing to the collective shadow, either that projected onto another or that projected by others? For instance, in making all-or-nothing demands such as on restricted access, to what extent are you adding fuel to your image as a Saboteur? What if you are able to make concessions, reprioritizing access restrictions only when it comes to nearing project go-live and after, so that end users can stress-test new modules without inhibition and arising bugs can be resolved expediently? In doing so, you are veering away from the Saboteur pole, and becoming closer to being a Partner to the implementation team. Conversely, how aware are you of your own projection of the Accomplice shadow on others? What if you saw them as enablers rather than detractors? To the extent that you have ideas of automating specific manual controls that take up an excessive amount of time both from control performance and validation perspectives, how can you, for instance, work with developers to introduce validity checks at appropriate intervals? From the perspective of building a robust system, you become partners in crime. Whether it is challenging the Saboteur collective shadow projected by others or acknowledging your own Accomplice collective shadow projected on others, you begin to notice the gradual blurring of boundaries between you and them. Relationships take on a more collegial tone, rather than reside behind he said/she said battle lines. Members from other implementation teams may even approach you on their own accord when debating various configuration options. The projected collective shadow conditions the way we behave towards one another. When the other is cast as a Saboteur or Accomplice, the same words, gestures, behaviors take on Saboteur or Accomplice undertones. To some extent, the collective shadow reflects a mental laziness of sorts, in which we pigeonhole individuals into neat, distinctive categories rather than take the time and effort to understand and connect with them.

In the remediation of audit deficiencies, auditors are often assigned the Critic or Observer collective shadows. From the perspective of the auditees, the auditors are quick to point out what went wrong to supervising management. Yet they never stayed long enough to undertake the real work of remediation. Come the next quarterly or annual audit, they turn up again to check up on the progress of remediation. Often, proposed improvements look good on paper, yet when it comes to implementing an additional detective review or tightening a system configuration, unexpected things can happen. Delays ensue when personnel designated as approvers are not able to review in a timely or complete manner. Transactions may need to be fixed on the backend if they remain stuck in interim processing queues with newly introduced configurations. The focus may be on remediating the identified deficiency at the cost of ignoring other risks. From the perspective of the auditors, auditees are assigned the Dogmatic or Authoritarian shadows. Auditees are perceived to be slow to adapt to change when it comes to implementing the proposed controls. They have seemingly a thousand and one excuses for not embracing a different approach. Or they appear too engrossed in, or distracted by, their daily work routines to carve out the time to internalize and execute any real improvement. Come the next audit update, remediation efforts are stalled; they seem only too keen to revert to the old way of getting things done.

As an auditor in this scenario, you have different ways to proceed. You can choose to contribute to the Dogmatic or Authoritarian shadow projected onto auditees. Or you can come to terms with the Dogmatic or Authoritarian shadows within your own group. By continuing to paint others as obstacles to change or progress, to what extent are you choosing not to see the dogma imposed by the audit guidance and workpapers you wield? To what extent are you overly Authoritarian in compelling auditees to put in place controls to ensure compliance without considering the impact on operational performance or customer satisfaction? In working with auditees, to what extent are you too motivated to complete the audit in a timely manner to roll up your sleeves in developing feasible solutions? Do your recommendations break or integrate with current processes? Do you even care? Are you no different from the Critic or Observer who shows up to shine a light on all that went wrong only to conveniently skip away when it comes time to get down to business? As auditors, we review, validate, assess. If we were to execute as well, this would compromise our objectivity. Yet, there is much that can be done without compromising this objectivity. We can explore how a proposed recommendation can best be executed, or possible interim workarounds to get us to the desired end state. We can ask what impact our proposal would have on existing operations and what new risks could arise from this change. Rather than cower behind our perceived Critic or Observer collective shadows, we can begin to walk the talk.

When we easily subscribe to the images we ascribe others, we also concede our individuality to the images others bestow upon us. Jung calls this a persona, "a mask that *feigns individuality*."[39] This is the heavy bag we each carry, as characterized by Bly, into which we dutifully deposit aspects of ourselves that confound or contradict established expectations. It is only by emptying the contents of this bag, stripping the mask of what we should be, that we start to awaken to the reality of who we are.

---

[39] Carl C. Jung, T*wo Essays on Analytical Psychology, The Collected Works of C. G. Jung*, Volume 7, Bollingen Foundation, New York, NY (1966), Second Edition, p.157.

Exercise

Look at the group you are a part of:

- To what extent are other groups a projection of their own collective shadow?
- To what extent is it in itself a reflection of a collective shadow of another group?

Look at your own role in your group:

- To what extent are you contributing to the collective shadow projected by others?
- To what extent are you contributing to the collective shadow your group projects onto others?

Identify ways you can retrieve the collective shadows projected:

- What if members of the other group presently join your group? How differently would you behave towards them?
- How would both sides behave if each loosens its grip on perceived intergroup boundaries or differences?
- What can you do to get to know individual members in the other group?

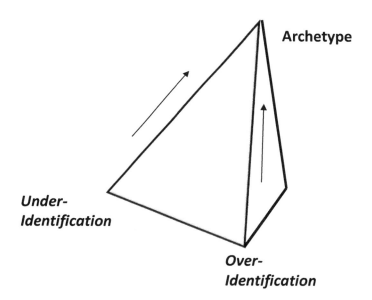

Figure 9: Balancing archetypal identification

Most of us are familiar with integrated audits where auditors, in addition to opining on financial statements, express an opinion on the effectiveness of a company's internal controls over financial reporting. Yet, how many of us are familiar with integrating our shadows?

As auditors, we are familiar with control self-assessment, where process owners perform tests of operating control effectiveness. Yet, how many of us perform periodic self-assessments of the archetypes we embody?

Table 7: Archetypal kleshas

Archetype	Shadow		Attachment	Aversion	Ignorance
Skeptic	Critic			■	
Skeptic	Dogmatic		■		
Sleuth	Interrogator			■	
Sleuth	Innocent				■
Protector	Authoritarian		■		
Protector	Observer				■
Partner	Accomplice		■		
Partner	Saboteur			■	

In Buddhism, *kleshas* are mental states that cloud the mind and manifest in unwholesome actions. Referred to as the three poisons in the Mahayana tradition, or three unwholesome roots in the Theravada tradition, the three *kleshas* of attachment, aversion, and ignorance are identified as the root or source of all other *kleshas*. Table 7 maps the shadow archetypes we have identified to its underlying *klesha* or hindrance.

When we think of attachment, the first *klesha*, a clinging of sorts comes to mind. From this perspective, it is easy to see how the vein of attachment can run through the Dogmatic, Authoritarian, and Accomplice shadow archetypes. The auditor as Dogmatic clings to established audit guidance and refuses to veer from the agenda. The auditor as Authoritarian clings to established internal controls and enforces these on new systems or functions that come into audit scope. The auditor as Accomplice clings to established relationships and begins to lose the necessary objectivity to provide unbiased insight. In addition to sharing this same clinging attribute, each shadow archetype shares the same outcome. With the auditor as Dogmatic, the desired outcome is adherence with tried and true guidelines. With the auditor as Authoritarian, the desired outcome is compliance with hitherto established controls. With the auditor as Accomplice, the desired outcome is maintenance of long-standing relationships. Clinging happens when there is something to cling to. Whether that may be guidance, process, or relationship, each of these shadow archetypes demonstrates a resistance to change. When we peel back yet another layer, this resistance reveals an underlying fear, fear of a different way, a different system, a different outcome.

Imagine a state of non-attachment. Have you ever been so immersed in an audit that you appear to lose all conception of time? As unexpected things crop up, you respond and incorporate them, all the time sustaining a healthy level of skepticism even to that of your own methodology. In tests of controls, I often find myself entertaining different approaches to test sampling. Depending on whether your unit of analysis is at the program line, function, module, or batched release level, your test samples differ. When auditees offer alternative approaches to mitigate risks, you welcome these as fresh, new suggestions from folks who do the work and know firsthand the pulse at the ground level. Preventive controls may appear preferable in theory but may slow things down in reality. In working through different options with stakeholders, the auditor may arrive at a solution that can improve the way we manage risks as well as speed up the way things get done. When you explore a new way of doing, one that may appear to threaten the very assumptions sustaining an existing auditor–auditee relationship, your client may appreciate you all the more for your forthrightness and dedication. Regardless of outcome, when you are immersed wholeheartedly in what you are doing, becoming at one with the audit, you pay less attention to the outcome, and more attention to the task at hand. Ironically, the less you force a particular outcome, the more likely you arrive at a real solution.

Aversion, the second *klesha*, elicits different images: disagreement, opposition, avoidance. In this respect, the Critic, Interrogator, and Saboteur archetypes all embrace different facets of aversion. You can tell from the manner an audit is performed that the auditor as Critic is at work. Aversion is also all too apparent in the manner the auditor as Interrogator shapes her interviews into a sledgehammer. A less obvert form of aversion underscores the behavior of the auditor as Saboteur when she provides a voice of dissent invariably at the wrong place and wrong time. When we peel back this layer of aversion, what emerges is a certain disregard for how things are as opposed to how they should be. Ironically, behind every vehement assertion lies indifference, feigned passion for what really is an insipid lack of interest in what the auditee has to say or do. Whereas the shadow archetypes sharing the attachment *klesha* care about and defend their position compulsively, the shadow archetypes sharing the aversion *klesha* really do not to care at all. Had they cared, they would have investigated deeper into what they perceive as undesirable in their auditees. During this inquiry, they would ask: why am I so opposed to what I'm seeing? How could this be a reflection of what I see in myself? What am I afraid of losing? What do I have to lose? If they did care, they might consider stepping outside of their own skin, however briefly. In doing so, they may see in their auditees' eyes the very traits that they are so vehemently against. To the auditor embodying the Critic, Interrogator, and Saboteur shadow archetypes, the auditees can all appear critical, demanding, or conniving. The reverse, however, can be said of how they in turn appear to their auditees: uninspiring, unreasonable, and uncooperative. There is also an implicit consensus in the game of us-versus-them: every auditor as Critic finds an opposing foil in the auditee as a Dogmatic, every auditor as a Saboteur faces her counter-opposite in the auditee as an Accomplice. Thus, feigned passion is not only a masquerade for indifference; it is also a cover-up behind what is really a shared complicity in playing the game of opposites.

Imagine a different scenario, one where we cease playing the game. There is no need to abide by the rules of the game because there is no game. For every critical aspect we see in the auditee, we are able to identify its counterpart in ourselves. When we feel that auditees are not responding in a timely manner to our requests for information, we are also able to see how we are not giving them adequate lead time when swooping in at yet another inopportune time to perform a periodic audit. For every hesitance we sense when interrogating stakeholders, we are only too cognizant of our inner wrestling and deliberations when it comes to providing an opinion on the state of controls. When it comes to rendering our opinion, how often do we worry about making the wrong recommendation? To what extent do recurring audit findings have more to do with our inability to target root causes and go beyond formulaic solutions than with auditee lapses in concentration and execution? For every self-serving auditee process we wish to subvert, are we just as aware of how accustomed we have grown to existing audit techniques? During SOX compliance, some auditors were so bent on obtaining physical signoffs that they were oblivious to other evidential forms of management oversight such as actual changes resulting from in-depth reviews. When we recognize others in ourselves, and ourselves in others, aversion becomes irrelevant, more akin to teenage angst and self-annihilation than any worthwhile adult endeavor.

In theory, ignorance, the third *klesha*, is what an audit is intended to overcome: ignorance of risks, of interdependencies, and of change. And yet, one often hears, "auditors, what do they know?" Stories abound on how auditees clean up shop just in time for a scheduled audit only to revert to disarray upon the auditor's exit. Both the Innocent and Observer shadow archetypes tap into ignorance. The auditor as Innocent takes what the auditee says or does at face value and looks no further. The auditor as Observer hovers in and out, content to point a finger from the sidelines and claiming no real accountability for helping improve the way work gets done. Compared to their active Interrogator and Authoritarian counterparts, these passive shadow archetypes are energy draining. When we peel back and look beneath, we see a lack of confidence in an ability to make a change or difference. Along with lack of self-confidence, self-doubt and ambivalence make good travelling companions. Let's peel back another layer. Could there be a lurking obsession with the ego or the self? How would we appear if we spoke up? What if we said something insanely inane? Would it not be better that we not speak up at all?

What if we put aside all attempts to appear credible? We can start by listening. Not just for what auditees say, but also for what they do not say. The lull between words can be revealing; what they do not say can tell us more than what they do say. Clients can, and often do, launch headlong into the slew of controls they have amassed. What they may fail to mention is the little time devoted to updating the requisite risk assessment that justifies these very controls in the first place. Putting aside credibility also means not being afraid to ask questions. I often encounter clients who are quick to issue dismissive remarks such as "that goes without saying," or "we would have thought about this" but upon further inquiry revisit their initial assumptions. Often this requires a certain level of thick skin not unlike that of an elephant's. It is for this very reason that I tell folks that auditing is a character building exercise. Yet, by playing the fool – whether it is through active listening or asking – you end up being anything but.

Much like how *kleshas* are seen as roots of suffering, our journey through auditor archetypal shadow and light is a process that is focused on snipping away at the root or the source. Rather than fall prey to their firm grip, this process demands that we accord some distance between ourselves and the personalities we cultivated over time. Awakening to our true potential does not have to entail meditating before a scared shrine surrounded by countless flickering candles (and falling asleep in the process). It may mean something as commonplace as taking a bus to work and recognizing that the archetypes you embody are like the different characters that get on and get off the bus. Clinging onto any one particular archetype would be like preventing a certain passenger from alighting. When the bus gets crowded, as it almost always does on my way to and from work, you can run into different characters, some appealing, others far less so. They jostle, leave you alone, or with so much as a friendly nod or wink, are gone sooner than you realize. Archetypes are like that. As auditors, we are predisposed to judging. The *kleshas* or hindrances remind us of the dangers of self-consciousness. As Masao Abe puts it, "we become involved in and limited by the distinction between self and others ... distinction turns into opposition, conflict, and struggle."[40] The storehouse consciousness in Buddhism has been compared to Jung's collective unconscious. The *skandhas* described in Chapter 5 are the means in which individual consciousness is created successively through form, sensation, perception, memory, and knowing. Our behaviors are conditioned by our thoughts, our thoughts by our minds.

When we project our shadow onto someone else, we look to him or her to take on that archetype. In becoming accustomed with relating to folks carrying our shadow, we unintentionally seek them out. An auditor who ignores her Critic shadow is more likely to encounter critical client

---

[40] Masao Abe, *Zen and Western Thought*, University of Hawaiian Press, Hawaii (1985).

after critical client. She undergoes the ups-and-downs characterized with handling a critical client. Why is she not aware of a new update to the audit guidance? Why has she not been able to complete the audit much sooner? Why were specific areas left out of scope? If she were a junior auditor, a critical audit manager may take the place of a critical client. Until she acknowledges her shadow, however, she will be reminded of it time and again. Most of us lead busy jam-packed lives, blissfully unaware of our inner trappings. We get caught up in a loop, riding the emotional rollercoaster each time. Over time, some of us become resigned and start to turn a blind eye. "Clients, what can you do?" we lament. Others become weary, helpless as they watch their power diminish with each passing day. In the example of the auditor who projects her Critic shadow, she may "learn" over time to immerse herself in administrative matters, leaving the deeper, richer endeavors in root-cause analyses to her perceived critics.

When we project our shadow onto someone else, something else happens. We draw distinctions: this versus that, us-versus-them. The other takes on one-dimensional black or white cardboard characters. Once a critic, always a critic. The auditor in our example may not say this aloud but her responses reveal otherwise. A simple question, change in tone, mere nuance on the part of the other is interpreted as yet another stab at criticism. Inevitably, an impasse is reached. The auditor may confront her client or audit manager. Or she may go through a visible breakdown of sorts. The client or audit manager reacts in disbelief: I was merely trying to help, I didn't mean to sound critical. Upon hearing this, the auditor may just yet realize that she has been battling her inner demon all this time. By facing her inner Critic, she can begin the work of channeling this energy into a healthy level of skepticism. Attention to detail, careful discrimination, receptivity to alternatives, all these attributes are useful in the course of an audit. In excess, they turn away the client; in their absence, the audit becomes a check-the-box exercise. The key is moderation.

A danger with dabbling in archetypes is the promise of an idealized slice of reality, what should or ought to be rather than what is. In aspiring to an ideal version of ourselves, we become self-conscious. It is like humming a favorite tune to yourself before realizing that you are being watched all this time. What happens? You freeze in your tracks and drop your tune. Out goes spontaneity. In performing her fieldwork, the auditor tenses, poised on a perpetual lookout for danger signs. To be an effective auditor, you need to be this and that. If the client does this, it could mean this or that. One's professional life becomes a long, drawn out, conditional affair. The inherent emptiness of things, the nature of dependent arising – these are intended to preclude an excessive attachment to perceived lines dividing us and others, shoring up unchanging, stale identities in need of airing out, to say the least. A fixation on attaining a specific idealized archetype is in itself an attachment no less. Until we realize that all else is malleable and whatever that we are so accustomed to cling onto is in itself a dependency, we would never be able to internalize the rationale for change, let alone attain the carefree abandon enjoyed by Chuang Tzu's butterfly. Through the process of awareness and letting go, we can start to loosen the hold of enveloping archetypes. The auditor as Protector knows enough to loosen up and revisit prior controls with newfound skepticism for assumptions that have long outlasted their utility. The auditor as Partner knows enough when favorable relations are beginning to blind her from objective insight.

A fixation on attaining idealized archetypes also forces our shadows deeper underground where they continue to fester and build up potency. If coming to terms with our interdependent reality is the first step, coming face to face with our shadow is surely a necessary second step. First emptiness, then pitch black darkness, "double negatives," as Siroj Sorajjakool points out.[41] Whether this is a shadow that we project onto another, or a group, we need to resist the urge to flee and come to terms with what seems dank, dark, or hideous. Robert Bly calls this process "retrieving our projection" or "eating our shadow."[42] We start to see ourselves in what we shun or despise in others. The auditee as silent Observer or client as conspiring Accomplice – these only serve to sensitize us to aspects of ourselves that we have hitherto chosen to bury.

It is through the slow simmer of everyday recognition and soul searching that we break through the shadow's hold over us. By projecting our inner Observer or Accomplice shadow onto others, we are likely to see ourselves as Protectors imbued with a sense of responsibility. Our words and actions, however, carry false conviction over the dichotomy we draw between us and them. We are more likely to encounter auditees who are Observers or Accomplices – think of scenes involving recurring audit findings or check-the-box audits – to whom we can ascribe

---

[41] Siroj Sorajjakool, *Do Nothing: Inner Peace for Everyday Living*, Templeton Foundation Press, US (2009).
[42] Robert Bly, *A Little Book on the Human Shadow*, HarperOne, Australia (June 1988).

the blame. We are also not facing our Observer or Accomplice shadow within. In the overall scheme of things, we continue to imprison ourselves in a fixed Protector stance. How then is it possible to bridge compliance with performance or security? Any enhancement that is intended to speed up an existing process becomes automatically subsumed under the umbrella of disdain: what of potential risks that could be bypassed? Good luck with trying to improve the compositional mix of automated over manual controls. Conversely, we are just as likely to miss the other side of the picture: how our audit recommendations – different flavors of password controls for different systems – can hinder work or impose externality costs such as burdening helpdesk to reset easily forgotten complex passwords.

This is possibly why audit conference topics such as "Delivering Value-Added Audits" continue to draw hundreds. We are forever held captive by that which we have prevented ourselves from attaining. My transitions from consulting to business analysis, business analysis to auditing, auditing to compliance, and compliance to systems implementation offer plenty of fodder for coming face to face with my shadows. Process flowcharts, procedures, tightened security – these are bread-and-butter constructs that I expect from clients as an auditor; in the midst of system implementations, these are re-prioritized against other endeavors such as encouraging user adoption or testing of new modules. Much like "eating my shadow," time and again, I have had to eat my own words. Audit recommendations that have been issued without missing a beat – periodic segregation of duties system access reviews – become cause for contemplation in light of the gargantuan time and effort involved in compiling an elegant segregation of duties report from legacy and new-age cloud applications alike, never mind getting the requisite mix of folks in the same room to perform a more than cursory review. Tying receipts and bills to their originating purchase orders in Procure-to-Pay is a recommended best practice but this does not account for actual user behavior. What if users submitted purchase requests for already received purchases? What if vendor bills were created separately from purchase orders? Can the system in turn correlate the two after the fact? A chasm exists between what should work and what actually works.

Our own shadow can be difficult to swallow. As an auditor transitioning from compliance audits to system pre-implementation reviews, I was quick to blame implementation consultants when things went awry. How could they not understand our needs? Did they not care? Were they not capable of configuring the system? It was not until I had to step in to validate system configurations and perform sandbox testing of transactions against ongoing master data updates that I began to appreciate hidden system complexities. All this time I had been blaming others, I was really refusing to acknowledge my own unfamiliarity and lack of in-depth knowledge of the system at hand. It was much easier to deflect – point the finger at someone else – than to look within.

Upon facing our shadow, what then? Changing long-standing behavioral patterns is no easier than acknowledging our shadow. It is like asking us to walk backwards or write with our left hand when we are right-handed. One of the things I found myself clinging on to was an aversion to things that went wrong. I would come home dejected over the seeming lack of progress made and mounting obstacles that cropped up each day. When in compliance, my role was to ensure that all the "i"s were dotted and "t"s crossed. In a system pre-implementation review with aggressive timelines, things were anything but; I would be lucky if there was time to get to housekeeping fundamentals. I would look at others in my role and wonder at how they were able to thrive on ambiguity and change. Were they any less accountable? Did they not care? Were they simply oblivious or unresponsive to client needs? Upon closer reflection, it occurred to me that they were none of these things. The key difference lay in their playful manner in exploring possibilities – alternate ways of doing things – leaving no stone unturned. Although I had left compliance, I was still stuck in compliance rewind. In my daily interactions with others, everything was fraught with tension; a simple error or omission was tantamount to failing an audit in my mind's eye. I had only to look to the camaraderie of my peers to realize that I was my own worst enemy.

My own experience speaks to the inner machinery of the mind. In spite of the arduous process we have taken towards acknowledging and accepting our shadow, our minds can still play tricks on us by hoodwinking us into thinking that we are loosening our hold of a specific archetypal pattern. The auditor as Authoritarian seeks to release her fear of vulnerability by striving even harder to make herself, and others, perfect. Whilst she has acknowledged and accepted her Authoritarian shadow, she has yet to accept her underlying fear of losing control and appearing vulnerable. The release that she seeks is not so much a release from the Authoritarian shadow as it is a flight from her own fears. She throws herself harder into her work, winding herself in an ever tightening bind of angst.

To release my Authoritarian shadow, I had first to release my need to control every detail, obsessing about getting things right the first time. By doing so, I was releasing my need to resolve every hiccup that arises. Second, I had to release holding myself to impossible standards. By doing so, I was able to release my fear of appearing ignorant, incompetent, or wrong. Third, I worked on releasing the expectation that there was only one right way of getting things done. By doing so, I could release myself from being the role of the cop, always on the lookout for something to go awry, ever ready to pounce. It was only by releasing myself from these three fears that I was finally able to release others from having to control every detail, aspire to impossible standards or conform to a singular approach of getting things done. We cannot leap from acknowledgement to acceptance and release in a single bound.

As my experience illustrates, my own release of my shadow has taken place on various levels. Yet, it is only by being willing to perform the hard work on oneself that one begins to listen to what others have to say, entertain differences in opinion or approach. By stepping outside of the Authoritarian shadow, I was able to release an over-identification with the Protector archetypal energy and begin the process of welcoming the Partner archetype in the system pre-implementation review.

Someone who is ready for everything, who doesn't exclude any experience, even the most incomprehensible ... will himself sound the depths of his own being[43]

---

[43] Rainer Maria Rilke, *Letters to a Young Poet*, Norton, New York (1962).

What happens when we do not know which archetype to tap into? As Jung put it, "we are well aware of what we have been, but we are not aware of what we are going to be."[44] Coming to terms with our shadow is one thing; most of us are still in the process of figuring out the path to take to realize our purpose in life. We must be careful, however, not to use this as an excuse to remain stuck in the familiar confines of an existing archetype. Ask yourself: would you rather remain sure about the boundaries you have erected or right about embracing possibilities for change? Would you rather be consistent in your public persona or adaptive in the manner you respond to a situation? As auditors, we are susceptible to the appeal of controls. Yet, when it comes to transcending auditor archetypes, we need to ask ourselves: to what extent does our desire to be in control preclude us from fulfilling our full potential? To what extent does our need to be right lead us astray on to the wrong path? A first step towards figuring out the right path is to see that we are truly deserving of the right path. When transitioning from compliance audits to system pre-implementation reviews, I was able to listen to what others have to say after I sought out my own voice. I was able to grant others the right to having differing opinions after I released myself from complying with exacting standards. As auditors, skepticism comes easily to us. Yet skepticism can slice both ways. We can be skeptical about a stale arrangement that has outlasted its utility, and with good reason. We can also be skeptical of new, unexplored territory. When we are unsure of which archetype to awaken, we may sell ourselves short, retreating to the familiar assurance of old comforts rather

---

[44] C. G. Jung, *Analytical Psychology: Its Theory and Practice*, Pantheon Books, New York (1968), p. 22.

than take a risk in uncharted waters. When we choose to stay open and flexible, we also stay true to a dynamic sense of self, one that exists and adapts in relation to others.

Transcendence is liberation from transfixed archetypes. Too often, we mistake our convictions as a source of strength. As Jung put it, "the test of a firm conviction is its elasticity and flexibility; like every other exalted truth it thrives best on the admission of its errors.[45].As auditors, we are adept at seeking out the errors or omissions of others, much to their chagrin. Just how well are we able to see, accept, and thrive on our omissions or errors? Transcendence is not about denying or denigrating archetypes. It is about fleshing them out and, in the process, living our lives truly, fully, unreservedly. At any moment in time, we hold and are capable of invoking multitudes – varied archetypal responses applicable to the situation at hand. By deepening our capacity to respond, we become fully realized, complex, and dynamic individuals in our own right. Likewise, auditees from whom we have retrieved our shadows become more real, more likeable, and, in other words, more human. They appear less critical, less detached, and altogether more engaging. Less forced he-said-she said rigmaroles, auditor–auditee relationships become a source of learning and fulfillment. Looking back, I learned more from audit engagements where there were intense, frank, back-and-forth discussions, revisiting of assumptions, and continual refinement of less than perfect solutions. Transcendence is a process, not an end state. It can take years to realize and release our existing

---

[45] Carl G. Jung, "Psychotherapy and a Philosophy of Life", in *Collected Works 16: The Practice of Psychotherapy*, Princeton University Press, Princeton (1966).

projections, much less identify new ones, or rise above our public personas as humorless, pedantic number crunchers. Every now and then, however, we muster enough conviction to re-write the script.

Exercise

Tribal communities use rituals to emphasize rites of passage: the onset of puberty, the transition from daughter to mother, son to warrior, adult to elder. For many auditors, similar rites of passage are experienced when they rise up through the ranks: auditor to senior, senior to manager, manager to senior manager and making partner. The experimentation with untapped auditor archetypes is not unlike going through a ritual of sorts, one far more accessible though no less potent. Modern-day rituals we can perform need not be elaborate affairs localized to a specific time and place. Every day can be an invitation to working with our archetypes and shadows. My daily bus ride to work, for instance, serves as my own reminder of the transitory nature of archetypes. On a singular ride alone, I can encounter multiple characters. Just the other day, a fellow passenger tried to get my attention to fix an upturned collar, another shoved me aside whilst cussing that I was in her way. For those of us on short, rotational audit projects, each engagement brings with it a fresh new set of encounters, each a gentle reminder of the inherent emptiness and dependent arising behind every archetypal response.

In the corporate world, most of us think of professional training or team-building excursions as a means to revisit or unlearn old mannerisms. Yet, how often do we leave these events charged and ever ready to try a different approach only to regress to our old ways and means the next day, and the day after? Real change can only come about through small, almost infinitesimal, ways we choose to remind ourselves to drop our attachment, not give in to the tendency to solidify our perceptions and responses. Think about the little ways you can seek to remind yourself of the nature of archetypes in your everyday life. These can be:

- Meeting new faces on a new audit assignment
- Watching passers-by on a lunch break
- Observing exchanges in a group or company meeting
- Contrasting inter and intra group dynamics – us-versus-them.

Our shadows can be likened to the sediment that settles at the bottom of a glass of water. When arising events stir up the water, the sediment rises. Think about the little ways you can alert yourself to potential shadows, aspects of your personality that you have buried deep within or chosen to project onto others:

- Feeling hurt or upset over a seemingly trivial matter
- Developing an instinctive dislike or aversion to something or someone
- Taking sides or having to prove a point
- Making all-good or all-bad distinctions or judgments.

Think about the little ways you can remind yourself to shake off the grip of enveloping archetypes:

- Walking in the park during lunch
- Getting a mid-afternoon coffee
- Waiting to catch the train
- Waiting for your computer to reboot after crashing.

For me, washing my hands is a gentle reminder to loosen the grip of archetypal responses that have accumulated in the course of a day. When I feel I'm getting stuck, sense tension in my shoulders, or hear my voice take on a grating tone, I know to take a quick break. Letting go does not mean self-negation. At any point in time, we are presented with multiple choices: assert our beliefs, open up to alternate points of view, fall in line with group norms, experience insight. What we do, and perhaps more importantly, *how* we do, depends on whether we are ready to release our hold of preconceptions of how it ought to be.

By integrating how we apprehend, accept, and release our archetypal responses in mundane daily activities, we start to "play" with archetypes over time. An uncooperative auditee or a bad review can elicit a combative response just as easily as a client compliment or unexpected finding can evoke a sense of accomplishment. Rather than hang on to any specific response, we learn to let it go; go with the ebb and flow. Arising personalities and events and our corresponding responses are like moving clouds in the sky. Hanging on to any one specific hurt and corresponding archetypal response to assert one's identity is like clinging to any one specific cloud to characterize the sky. When we embrace the uncertainty in an audit, we become more fluid. We become less solemn, more light-hearted, less self-conscious, more engaged with who or what is at hand. We embark on the subtle everyday process of transcending IT auditor archetypes.

PART III: POSTSCRIPT

CHAPTER 9: NO SCRIPT

Figure 10: Beyond archetypes

Audit originates from the Latin word *audītus*, which means the sense or act of hearing. Yet, how many of us, in the face of looming deadlines and countless checklists, take the time to actually listen to our clients? Auditors and auditees need each other. Auditees rely on auditors to provide an honest, unbiased perspective on the current state of affairs. IT auditors, in particular, can provide a unique insight into the inner workings of a system that auditees in business and accounting domains are not privy to. In thinking about the role of auditors, I'm reminded of the *kōan*:

If a tree falls in a forest and no one is there, does it make a sound?

A *kōan*, in Zen Buddhism practice, is a riddle that presents one with a paradox. In the above *kōan*, one is presented with the question: without the listener, is there a sound? When extrapolated to auditing, one can posit: without the auditor, can one identify what went wrong?

But auditors also need the auditees in order to formulate, develop findings of value, meaning. Audit findings are not generic; excessive access, for instance, in one organization is not the same in another. Excessive access is interwoven with the behavioral patterns of personnel who transitioned to new roles, performed shadow support, or left the organization altogether. The auditor who is focused on herself, on what she needs to accomplish or how she appears to others, to sheer exclusivity, exhibits narcissism. The more she focuses on appearing capable or effective, the less capable or effective she becomes. The more she focuses on displaying her strengths, the more she is inclined to conceal her shadows. The archetypes presented in this book are not intended to be an unambiguous or exhaustive list; the reality is that there are as many archetypes as there are life circumstances. As an audit continues to present an auditor with unexpected surprises – things not working out as they should or appear to be – she needs to be careful not to develop a protective shield to screen out what might appear to be obstacles in her path but are really invitations to partake in life's complexities. A recurring audit finding does not necessarily mean uncooperative auditees; it can also mean that the initial proposed solution may sound good in theory but needs further refinement in practice. By continuing to stay open and connected to others, the auditor is also better able to recognize and integrate parts of herself she projects or suppresses. Inherent emptiness and dependent arising illustrate not only the interconnected world we live but also our relational selves.

As with all realities, the self is inherently relational. It is always in relation to other selves in the human community[46]

By closing ourselves to others, we are denying the very opportunities to come into our own being. When we cling to the attitude that auditees are ignorant or resistant to change, we remain closed to receiving new ideas or insight. The audit becomes a one-way street: the auditor chooses and gets to see what she would like to see; auditees know too well upon her exit that the real work has only just begun. When we revisit the four primary archetypes we covered in this book, it may help to identify in each a recurring pattern employed to confront the challenge at hand (see Table 8).

Table 8: Archetypal journeys

Archetype	Challenge	Objective
Skeptic	Inquire into what is accepted or unknown	Expose possibilities
Sleuth	Uncover the facts	Obtain clarity
Protector	Mitigate identified risks	Shore up defenses
Partner	Integrate efforts with other stakeholders	Obtain buy-in or consensus

---

[46] Neville Symington, *Narcissism: A New Theory*, Karnac Books, London (1993).

Each archetype bears its own fruit as it comes into being. Yet, as we continue in the progress of the audit, or in the growth of our professional careers, do we continue to tell ourselves the same story? The irony is that whilst embodying a particular archetype can help us attain a goal at a point in time, clinging onto it indefinitely can only hinder us in the process of becoming/coming into our own. In covering attachment as one of the three *kleshas*, we ask ourselves: when is enough *enough*? When does it make sense to give up identifying more defenses as a Protector or seeking more alternative perspectives as a Skeptic? Humility could be the very antidote to any smugness or conceitedness developed over time.

When we insist on our own separateness from others, we sabotage our own journeys. A crisis in the form of a dissatisfied audit client may eventually force us to acknowledge and release our own insecurities. As auditors, we spend much of our time convincing others who are keen to protect their turf. In understanding the archetypes we take on, and the shadows we project or suppress, we may yet realize that real work lies in first convincing ourselves to let go of our own turf. Just as we expend time and energy getting the auditees to confront their own fears of what can go wrong, we need to spend the same time and energy facing our own fears. As long we continue to see ourselves in isolation, or see auditees from an us-versus-them perspective, we will remain closed to our fundamental connectedness. Auditors in fast changing organizations do not decry the futility of their efforts to devise long-standing controls but embrace the challenge to keep in step with the rapid turn of events. Conversely, auditors in stable, mature organizations see their role as an agent of change. Events that transpire in the course of our audits serve to keep us in check. They remind us to integrate our shadows or competing archetypes. The auditor as a Partner can easily become an Accomplice without the Skeptic archetype. Until we can undergo an honest self-reflection, we will continue to blame others or run for cover. I am reminded of a Chuang Tzu narrative of a man who kept running away from his shadow without realizing that it would disappear if he only stepped into the shade. Nothing is inherently wrong with our shadows; what is amiss is our response to them. Just as some audit findings tend to recur time and again forcing us to dig deeper to identify more than surface solutions, we will encounter recurring issues or dramas as part of our archetypal growth. Progress takes on a spiral effect. As a senior auditor, we may see things in black and white. As we take on additional managerial responsibilities that come with being an audit manager, hard boundaries start to soften. At each leg of our journey, we may encounter different flavors of the Saboteur or Accomplice archetypal shadows as we continue to hone our ability to partner with our clients in developing sustainable audit solutions. For some of us, it can take as much time to come to terms with our shadows as it is to let go of them. As auditors, we are inclined to perform deep dives, engaging in root-cause analyses of what went, or could go, awry. By seeing our shadows as bipolar opposites in each of the four primary auditor archetypes, we are in a sense looking beyond surface symptoms. We are more likely to appreciate the hidden potential behind what appears on the surface. When encountering the Critic in an auditee, we are able to spot the Skeptic waiting in the wings. When coming face to face with the Critic in ourselves, we give ourselves the room to channel this into a healthy level of skepticism. Rather than react unconsciously to each archetypal behavior, we begin to recognize the fear of vulnerability behind the Authoritarian or the Critic's aversion towards uncertainty. By being patient with others, we are not writing them off. By being patient with ourselves, we are not condemning ourselves. The experience of one's shadow, such as the Interrogator, can be seen as a first step towards embodying the Sleuth archetype. Whilst the intent behind their actions is the same – both driven by a need to uncover the truth of the matter – the intensity varies.

When we do let go of our shadow, we may feel like we are stepping into the void. Yet in a sense, we have always existed in the void; the archetypes being inherently empty to begin with and existing in relation to others. The attachment *klesha* becomes a hoarding of empty space in our case. The exercises we complete at the conclusion of each chapter remind us that the archetype we embody cannot be easily pinpointed, if at all. Letting go is a step in the right direction toward a balancing of archetypes. Balancing is not about attempting to juggle all the archetypes simultaneously. It is about knowing how a specific archetype can come to the fore at any given moment in time. We may feel slighted by an auditee who deems us ignorant of real-life workarounds; it helps to recognize at this moment that our Innocent shadow is activated. Letting go does not mean repudiating our archetypes or cherry-picking the best one to display at any given moment. It is about uncovering their interrelatedness. In righting the balance, we are not so much burying the Innocent archetype as we are giving voice to other archetypes, the Sleuth and the Protector, to investigate viable options to mitigate risk. Righting the balance can be seen at a collective level where the pendulum swings from an absence of controls in the pre-Enron era to an excess of controls post-Enron and early SOX, to a delicate balance of the organization's risk appetite with key controls in the late SOX and Jobs Act era. By letting go of our preconceptions, our perception changes; we undergo a paradigm shift. As auditors, controls are our common currency. In transcending archetypes, we are really giving up the illusion of control to awaken to the true fullness of our being.

When awakening archetypes, are we acting in a carefree manner, flying hither and thither like the Chuang Tzu's butterfly, or are we weighed down by the burden of expectation? In our daily work, we can be easily deluded into thinking that our every action is intentional or autonomous, yet archetypes operate at a far deeper psychic level. The vacillation between what is real and what is a dream in Chuang Tzu's narrative alludes to this collective unconscious. For Jung, individuation is a lifelong process that we each undergo, integrating collective and individual elements, ultimately loosening our attachment to specific archetypes, the hold the collective unconscious wields over us. By acknowledging, releasing, and experimenting with various auditor archetypes in our daily interaction with others, we are really tapping into the fullness of our being. Is it any wonder, then, that in ancient Greek the word for butterfly is also psyche? The butterfly's path is an ongoing journey, with no definitive goal in sight. Likewise, there is no singular ultimate archetype to strive for, or social rungs to scale. In the words of novelist Margaret Atwood, "in Paradise, there are no stories, because there are no journeys."[47]

---

[47] Margaret Atwood, *The Blind Assassin*, McClelland and Stewart, Toronto (2000).

This book would not be complete without some coverage on the ways we can tap into specific archetypes. To be sure, we are each not immune to the effects of socialization whether through our immediate family context, our friends, professional colleagues, or the community we live in. Seen from this perspective, it may be immediately obvious as to why specific archetypes thrive whilst others continue to languish in obscurity. In an organization, individuals whose archetypes conflict with that of the collective may choose to stay, but are more likely to leave to join like-minded peers to develop collegial working relationships. Outside of work, professional organizations offer a space for sharing experiences and learning from one another. It helps to attend the talks organized; in a way, it gives one insight into the different archetypes that are not immediately apparent to one's frame of mind. As an auditor buried deep in the trenches attempting to complete a thousand and one tasks, it is not easy to excavate oneself from one's immediate context of deliverables and deadlines. Yet, when listening to a product manager present a security product or a chief audit executive explain the way she realigned the audit function to better support business units, one is momentarily transported out of one's own skin. Rather than see it as a way of acquiring concrete tips and techniques that are task-oriented, see how the product manager is embodying the Partner archetype or how the audit executive is embracing the Protector archetype. The key is not to try too hard to see how it would apply to one's context, but simply to absorb, soak it in. Changes do not take place overnight. Yet, by continuing to stay open, you may notice how, when discussing controls with the auditees, you may approach controls from a usability perspective and not just from a compliance one. When discussing potential solutions to a recurring audit deficiency, you may explore roping in unlikely allies from other functions, whose distributed entry points in an end-to-end process can double up as control checkpoints (see Figure 11).

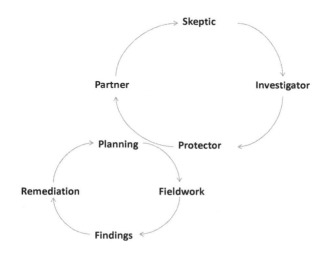

Figure 11: Archetypal and audit lifecycles

Whether through mentors or supervisors, most of us periodically receive feedback on our performance at work. What appears to be a simple observation – such as having to better run audit meetings – can take on different shades from an archetypal perspective. One can simply focus on the contents of the task: running an agenda, taking meeting notes, following up on tabled items. Or one can look at the manner in which the meetings are conducted. Is the Interrogator shadow archetype dominating the discussion so that any novel suggestion is instantly shut down to abide by the agenda at hand? In this case, the meeting may be run efficiently but its efficacy remains suspect. Alternatively, is the Accomplice shadow lurking beneath prior to one-on-one closed-door conversations leading up to the meeting? In acknowledging specific archetypes or shadows at work, one can start to address the underlying fears of uncertainty, vulnerability, or opposition. In a sense, the solution to better run meetings is not to simply focus on the mechanics of running a meeting but to own up to one's underlying motivations.

Auditors are fortunate enough to witness various levels of abstraction. Through interviewing an auditee, one may see how a backup is performed. Upon successful completion, one inspects an automated email notification. In reviewing disaster recovery or business continuity plans, one is able to understand how the backup would be retrieved to restore business operations. When compiling the results for a report to upper management, one distills the nature of the work performed to its essence and sheds light on how it contributes to the overall system of internal controls. In the same manner, archetypes can be viewed as varied levels or multiple facets of you. Whether you are actively conscious of this or not, you take on different archetypal roles – Skeptic, Sleuth, Protector, Partner – at different times. All of this happens organically so you may not even be aware of it. Yet, for some of us, we are confined to taking on the same archetype at an inopportune moment over and over again. It is like going too in-depth into the mechanics of performing actual data backup when presenting one's work to management each time. When we see archetypes in these terms, they become more accessible and hopefully easier to identify in the fabric of our everyday. A problem I see with simply relying on visualization as a means of activating a desired archetype is that it continues to be cut off from mundane reality. Taking time out to try to manifest the

Partner archetype for instance can seem like hocus pocus, and often does in retrospect when it results in delusion: one thinks one is a Partner when one's actions continue to reflect anything but. If, on the other hand, one is able to identify archetypal elements or shades in routine endeavors, one stands a better chance of either summoning or releasing requisite archetypal energies.

Changes in one's status at work can be a good means of gauging underlying archetypal play. When an auditor is promoted from a senior to a manager, she takes on responsibilities of a different nature. Rather than perform more of the same – fieldwork for instance – she is expected to manage a team and its deliverables as well as spend more time interfacing with audit management. Should her personality change dramatically when taking on this promotion, one is tempted to think that she has graduated onto a new archetype. Yet what could be just as likely is the surfacing of a repressed archetype. If she acts like an Authoritarian, it may be that in all the time leading up to her advancement, she has been depriving herself of the Protector archetypal energy. The promotion is but an outlet for repressed energy waiting to implode. A good gauge of archetypal energy is physical sensation. Are your shoulders tensed? Does your throat feel parched dry? Do you find it hard to pay attention to what others have to say? Ripening to the fullness of an archetype that aligns with the challenge at hand is not supposed to be a nerve-wrecking, anxiety-ridden experience. When you feel like you are on the edge, there is likely a lurking archetypal shadow. Auditing can be a grueling profession. Visiting different auditees or clients during the course of a single day, being prepared to rattle off different systems and the risks inherent in their use, responding to last-minute meetings to resolve unexpected issues, securing a workspace and network connectivity in an unfamiliar setting, these are part and parcel of an auditor's job. It is no wonder that many auditors are particularly susceptible to job burnout and attrition rates are not insignificant at Big Four accounting firms. Thus, it makes sense in soliciting specific archetypes that we focus not so much on the "what" but the "how." How we tap into the Protector archetype, for one, matters. Are we haranguing others through the Interrogator shadow? The more we press on, the less we accomplish. The less we gain, the more frustrated we become. Events may conspire to try to break our compulsion. An auditee may make a joke; an area that needs to be audited may no longer be applicable. Yet, when ensnared by the Authoritarian shadow, we feel compelled to press on, oblivious to even the most obvious stop sign.

What one really needs is to step outside of oneself. To this end, I have found *kōans* useful. *Kōan* is a Japanese rendering of the Chinese term Kung-An, or public cases. Originating from public cases belonging to Chán-masters in the Tang dynasty, *kōans* are a staple in the study of Zen. Typically phrased in the form of a perplexing riddle or paradox, *kōans* are intended to stop one's ceaseless flow of thoughts and provide a source for introspection. I am reminded of the *kōan* where, upon being paid a visit by a university professor, the Japanese master kept pouring his visitor's cup until it overflowed. When confronted, the master pronounced, "like this cup ... you are full of your own opinions and speculations."[48]

---

[48] Muju Ichien and Robert E. Morris, *Sand and Pebbles (Shasekishu): The Tales of Muju Ichien, A Voice for Pluralism in Kamakura*

As an auditor, do you step into every new situation with an open mind? Or are you more likely to arm yourself with a chock load of practice aides, checklists, and past experiences? How likely are you able to learn, let alone uncover new solutions or transcend archetypes? In looking back at my audit engagements, I have found that the ones I found most fulfilling are, ironically, the ones where I experienced the most pre-audit trepidation. I would study the particular intricacies of the systems in use beforehand. Yet, from the first day I arrived for onsite fieldwork through the course of the entire engagement, I took nothing for granted: I reached out to impacted stakeholders, asked, and, in some cases, reiterated questions to obtain clarification, and inspected various forms of evidence even ones that may be initially deemed out of scope. Because I knew no one, I listened intently to everyone. Because I had no prior assumptions, I was able to discern implicit beliefs and compare these with explicit actions. Because I had no insight into existing processes, I mapped them out from start to finish. Despite my condition of not knowing, I was more alert than ever. Not to sugarcoat the experience, there were many challenging days meeting less than familiar faces, remembering everyone's roles and names. Yet, when the engagement drew to a close, I was able to identify specific breaks lodged in key processes and systems. Unwittingly, the engagement and its challenges gave me an opportunity to explore and tap into the Sleuth and Partner archetypes to a greater degree. In the past, I had been content with embodying Skeptic and Protector archetypes in recurring engagements, inundated with prior case notes

---

Buddhism, SUNY Series in Buddhist Studies, State University of New York Press, New York (1985).

and workpapers. I was reminded of this *kōan* just the other day when someone asked me what my expectations were when transitioning to a new job. When I replied that I did not recall having any, she laughed, and said, "No, really."

I am reminded of another *kōan* where a student went to his master wishing to be rid of his temper. When asked to locate it, he could not produce it. To which the master explained, "then ... it must not be your own true nature."[49]

As with any challenging audit engagement, including the aforementioned one, tempers are easily frayed. It is easy to stay stuck in a specific stance, or archetype. How could the client management be so unyielding? Did they not understand that one had to perform all aspects from an audit from planning to fieldwork to analysis and compilation? How else did they expect one to proceed? It could take me a day, sometimes even a week, for feelings of self-righteousness to dissipate. I would distract myself to no end only to return the very source of my troubles. What helped for me over time was gaining a level of attentiveness to my feelings. Rather than run away from them or suppress them through a veneer of sheer positivity, I tried locating them. What was this rage that consumed my entire being to the point that I no longer paid attention to anything else or felt hunger? Where was it? Where did it go? Did it become fear? By paying attention to anger, I was neither fanning the fire nor putting it out. I was simply observing it for what it was. And soon enough, through this process, other thoughts, other feelings entered the picture. I started to see things from another point of view. I felt tired, not to mention hunger pangs. The self I was clinging to was but

---

[49] Muju Ichien and Robert E. Morris, Ibid.

one of the five *skandhas*; the anger was but a passing shower. By giving it up, I was also giving up my Interrogator shadow. By starting to reconnect what others said with what I have gathered, I realized that in my haste, I was not picking up obvious clues in piecing together the puzzle.

Between the beginning and ending stages of performing an audit, the auditor is beset by the constant danger of losing sight of the overall objective to mitigate risk. This loss can just as easily result from insisting on only seeing things her way as it can from accepting at face value varied opinions of multiple auditees. The point of the presented *kōans* is to remind us that the audit is a dynamic, ever-changing process. Prior workpapers, auditee experiences, best practices can, and often do, form the very basis upon which we start to explore our options, yet the outcome of an audit – its conclusions and recommendations – is invariably shaped by the conditions under which it is performed. When we see ourselves as multi-archetypal beings, we can better understand our roles as stewards guiding different inclinations, temperaments, and experiences within each of us towards a common goal. Contrary to popular belief, the audit is just as subject to inner demands, as it is to the outer demands of compliance and regulations.

In undertaking this journey through auditor archetypes, we have drawn on multiple disciplines encompassing psychology and philosophy. These are not run-of-the-mill topics you find on training agendas in audit conferences. I invite you to suspend any momentary disbelief or discomfort experienced.

9: No Script

If I may present a Chuang Tzu quote[50]:

The purpose of words is to convey ideas. When the ideas are grasped, the words are forgotten

Labels, paradigms, archetypes – these are but means that help us get to the root, the source. Regardless of what you believe, to quibble over the means is to miss the forest for the trees. The *kōans*, for instance, urge us to look within ourselves. What is this self? Where is it? We have seen how our minds can project or create their own illusions and realities. In a famous section of his "*Genjōkōan*," Master Dōgen wrote: "To study the self is to forget the self. To forget the self is to be enlightened by all things of the universe." When we study ourselves, we forget ourselves. What happens when we put ourselves aside, step outside of ourselves? What remains? Everything else: others, trees, land, the universe. What are these selves that we cling to but walls that separate us from everything else? When we examine auditor archetypes, we are looking within: what archetype is dominant and what archetypes lie beneath? To study archetypes is thus to see through their inherent emptiness, their interdependent realities.

To study auditor archetypes is to forget auditor archetypes. To forget auditor archetypes is to step out of archetypes that act like closed doors to our universal experience. To forget auditor archetypes is to open up to the audit universe: the interconnectedness amongst auditors and auditees, the interplay amongst audit, operating performance and enterprise security. This is nothing short of transcendental.

---

[50] Thomas Merton, *The Way of Chuang Tzu*, New Directions, New York (1969).

ITG RESOURCES

IT Governance Ltd. sources, creates and delivers products and services to meet the real-world, evolving IT governance needs of today's organizations, directors, managers and practitioners.

The ITG website (*www.itgovernance.co.uk*) is the international one-stop-shop for corporate and IT governance information, advice, guidance, books, tools, training and consultancy.

Other Websites

Books and tools published by IT Governance Publishing (ITGP) are available from all business booksellers and are also immediately available from the following websites:

www.itgovernance.eu is our euro-denominated website which ships from Benelux and has a growing range of books in European languages other than English.

www.itgovernanceusa.com is a US$-based website that delivers the full range of IT Governance products to North America, and ships from within the continental US.

www.itgovernanceasia.com provides a selected range of ITGP products specifically for customers in the Indian sub-continent.

www.itgovernance.asia delivers the full range of ITGP publications, serving countries across Asia Pacific. Shipping from Hong Kong, US dollars, Singapore dollars, Hong Kong dollars, New Zealand dollars and Thai baht are all accepted through the website.

Toolkits

ITG's unique range of toolkits includes the IT Governance Framework Toolkit, which contains all the tools and guidance that you will need in order to develop and implement an appropriate IT governance framework for your organization. For a free paper on how to use the proprietary Calder–Moir IT Governance Framework, and for a free trial version of the toolkit, see:

www.itgovernance.co.uk/calder_moir.aspx.

There is also a wide range of toolkits to simplify implementation of management systems, such as an ISO/IEC 27001 ISMS or an ISO/IEC 22301 BCMS, and these can all be viewed and purchased online at *www.itgovernance.co.uk*.

Training Services

IT Governance offers an extensive portfolio of training courses designed to educate information security, IT governance, compliance, and audit professionals. Our class room and online training program will help you develop the skills required to deliver best practice, compliance, and audit advice to any organization. They will also enhance your career by providing you with industry standard certifications and increased peer recognition. Our range of courses offers a structured learning path from Foundation to Advanced level in the key topics of Information security, IT governance, business continuity, and service management.

We offer a number of Management System Lead Auditor training courses which provide delegates with the practical knowledge required to plan and execute audits in line with the requirements of an ISO standard. These include the ISO27001 Certified ISMS Lead Auditor and ISO22301 Certified BCMS Lead Auditor training courses. Delegates who successfully complete these courses are awarded Certified Lead Auditor qualifications by the International Board for IT Governance Qualifications (IBITGQ).

Full details of all IT Governance training courses can be found at *www.itgovernance.co.uk/training.aspx*.

Professional Services and Consultancy

IT Governance's expert consultants can guide the development of IT auditing skills within your organization. We understand the various IT auditor archetypes and can show you, through mentoring and coaching, how to develop a richer, fuller, auditing practice.

We can help you to avoid the misconception that being effective means being critical and confrontational, and instead show you how to break free of any ascribed auditing roles or stereotypes.

With our support, you can learn to re-examine your own inner paradigms from a third-person standpoint, thereby opening your view to a plethora of perspectives.

Through the benefit of our extensive IT auditing experience, you can pick up the contextual clues in the client environment, and find allies in the process of augmenting internal controls – achieving full compliance with regulations and standards, and ensuring that your IT serves the organization and its customers.

For more information about IT Governance's Consultancy Services see

www.itgovernance.co.uk/consulting.aspx.

ITG Resources

Publishing Services

IT Governance Publishing (ITGP) is the world's leading IT-GRC publishing imprint that is wholly owned by IT Governance Ltd.

With books and tools covering all IT governance, risk and compliance frameworks, we are the publisher of choice for authors and distributors alike, producing unique and practical publications of the highest quality, in the latest formats available, which readers will find invaluable.

www.itgovernancepublishing.co.uk is the website dedicated to ITGP enabling both current and future authors, distributors, readers and other interested parties, to have easier access to more information. This allows ITGP website visitors to keep up to date with the latest publications and news.

Newsletter

IT governance is one of the hottest topics in business today, not least because it is also the fastest moving.

You can stay up to date with the latest developments across the whole spectrum of IT governance subject matter, including; risk management, information security, ITIL® and IT service management, project governance, compliance and so much more, by subscribing to ITG's core publications and topic alert emails.

Simply visit our subscription centre and select your preferences: *www.itgovernance.co.uk/newsletter.aspx*.

EU for product safety is Stephen Evans, The Mill Enterprise Hub, Stagreenan, Drogheda, Co. Louth, A92 CD3D, Ireland. (servicecentre@itgovernance.eu)

www.ingramcontent.com/pod-product-compliance
Lightning Source LLC
Chambersburg PA
CBHW071129050326
40690CB00008B/1397